795

DATE DUE

	15 me	
GRAB MAR 19 '90		
GAYLORD		PRINTED IN U.S.A.

BETTINA HÜRLIMANN

Picture-Book World

TRANSLATED AND EDITED BY BRIAN W. ALDERSON

Modern picture-books for children from twenty-four
countries with a bio-bibliographical supplement by Elisabeth
Waldmann

THE WORLD PUBLISHING COMPANY
CLEVELAND AND NEW YORK

Published by The World Publishing Company
2231 West 110th Street, Cleveland, Ohio 44102

First published 1965 under the title *Die Welt im Bilderbuch* by Atlantis Verlag, Zürich

© 1965 Atlantis Verlag AG, Zürich
English translation © Oxford University Press 1968. First published in this edition 1968

First United States Edition 1969
Library of Congress Catalog Card Number 69–13066

Colour plates and half-tone reproductions printed in Switzerland by Druck Lüthi & Co.

Printed in Great Britain by Fletcher & Son Ltd, Norwich

Contents

The Age for Picture-Books

A little girl, for whom I have a great affection, comes to see me every week. When she called today we settled down together to make a picture. I took some coloured paper and cut out a square, and this was a house, then a four-legged shape, and this was a horse, then a pair of two-legged figures holding hands, and these were the man and woman who lived in the house; then we stuck down some green snippings so that the horse could eat some grass. Together we went on cutting and tearing, taking it in turns to lick the sticky side of the paper, until eventually we had a whole world in front of us. We had a brightly coloured cloud and a sun for the day, and a dark cloud and a moon for the night, and we had a big piece of blue paper with some yellow bits scattered on it, and these were the wild ducks swimming on our own Lake Zürich.

In a single hour we lived through days and nights. We had a summer garden with all its animals and birds; and then to finish we put the little girl herself into it with her two cousins, despite the fact that they live on the other side of the world. In this way we conjured up real life on to our paper and the picture itself worked a remarkable magic in return.

Now, with the little girl packed off to bed, I have to settle down at my desk to write my introduction to this survey of modern picture-books from all quarters of the globe. What is more, it ought to be about the most beautiful picture-books—but what precisely are these? A day or two ago I thought I still knew, but now I am extremely doubtful. Everywhere prizes are being awarded to those books with the handsomest pictures, the most original ideas, the most refined graphic processes—and even with the best educational aims. They are all here in front of me, magnificent pictures of everything you can think of—from the Heavenly Father Himself to a flea under a microscope. Their splendour defies description, wrapped between glossy laminated jackets—the world in pictures and pictures from all round the world.

The little girl has already had a foretaste of these riches. Here and there she has been helped to a new sight of the world, and a picture has shown her something which was only half understood in the brief verses of a nursery rhyme. Many things seen here in their perfection may well have developed from the kind of primitive shapes which we were gluing together in our picture today, and in my selection of illustrations I have consistently tried to bear in mind the spontaneous relationship that should exist between author, illustrator, and child. By doing this I have made sure that wherever this relationship occurs, the child's understanding should also be taken into account, even when it is a question of almost abstract phenomena making up the pictures, as in the book where two children are represented only by a couple of coloured blobs. Obviously a child will understand more easily mice or bears depicted with minute accuracy down to the hairs in their tails or the wrinkles in their ears, but either way, abstract or representational, the danger lies in technique for technique's sake or a striving for graphic effects, for then the pictures will lose that magic which will always live in the crude world of sticky paper which we created today.

The little anecdote at the beginning of this preface seems to me to be a better way of clarifying our intentions for this book than a lot of theoretical pronouncements. In the following survey of some of today's most artistically satisfying picture-books we have tried hard not to forget the children who have to look at them.

Naturally this does not just mean one little girl for whom a few sticky shapes cut out by her grandmother take on so much significance. It includes also those older and, in matters of art, more sophisticated children for whom pictures do not simply take the place of words but accompany them and interpret them. For these children increasing weight must be given to the method of representation as well as to spontaneity and sincerity. This 'method' is a thing subject to many kinds of rule and various ways of classification; but since it is not our wish to provide here either a technical or a psychological handbook but rather to bear witness to the variety of work that is being done in the 'picture-book world', we have allowed artistic quality in almost every case to tip the balance.

I hope that this book will also show some of my gratitude to the many artists all round the world who are not too proud to devote the best part of their talents to giving pleasure and a richer experience to children.

BETTINA HÜRLIMANN

An introduction to the picture-book anthology, with acknowledgements, is given on pp. 59–60.

An asterisk * following the name of an illustrator indicates that an article on that person will be found in the alphabetical sequence of biographies at the end of the book.

Ota Janeček, «Z Modré Konvičky Prší na Žofín», Praha 1962

Picture-Books in German-Speaking Countries

Picture-books in Germany have a venerable history which dates back to such learned children's books as Basedow's *Elementarwerk* (Berlin, 1770–74) and to such prodigious, almost encyclopaedic, compilations as Bertuch's *Bilderbuch* (Weimar, 1796). One could even place the *Orbis pictus* of Comenius among the forbears of the German picture-book, for it was first published at Nuremberg in 1658. And indeed, Nuremberg, along with Berlin and Neu Ruppin, was also a centre for the *Bilderbogen*, or picture broadsheets, which catered to children's amusement from the eighteenth century onwards.

In the nineteenth century such outstanding illustrators as Theodor Hosemann, Otto Speckter, Ludwig Richter, Oskar Pletsch, and Franz Pocci brought into their pictures something of the spirit of fairy-tale and nursery rhyme, while later on, through their collaboration in the *Münchner Bilderbogen*, they gave a branch of popular journalism a new standard of quality. The real revolution, however, that against didacticism in children's books, was led by Dr. Heinrich Hoffmann with his *Struwwelpeter* (Frankfurt, 1845) and his five later picture-books. These were to be followed from 1864 onwards by the cautionary epics in pictures by Wilhelm Busch.

The end of the century saw a second revolution take place led by Heinrich Wolgast, whose movement for education through art demanded that children's books should also be works of art. This coincided with new developments in colour printing which made larger editions possible and led to the commercialization of the picture-book. In this way an opposition which had scarcely been present before sprang up between those children's books manufactured only for profit and picture-books of a predominantly artistic character. From now on the products of the so-called 'picture-book factories' with their quota of novelty books and popular oleograph literature stood in direct contrast to those picture-books produced by more delicate processes and imbued with a sense of artistic form.

Today this opposition is largely resolved. Criticism is mostly in the hands of the new disciples in the movement for education through art—such people as teachers and the assessors on examination boards—and the way is open for truly worthwhile picture-books. As a rule excellence is recognized and its claims furthered by both critics and educationists.

One of the moderns from the first half of this century was Karl Hofer who, as a young painter before the First World War, illustrated the picture-book *Rumpumpel* with text by Paula Dehmel (Cologne, 1903). (A similar children's book, *Fitzebutze*, by her husband Richard Dehmel, had been illustrated in 1900 by the painter-poet Ernst Kreidolf.) *Rumpumpel* created a storm of the

8

first order among painters and encouraged many professional artists to undertake similar work. The Cologne publishing house of Schaffstein was the centre for these to some extent experimental activities, and in 1904 an extremely interesting collection of poems, *Buntscheck*, was issued. This was illustrated by Freyhold, Kreidolf, Karl Hofer, and several other artists now forgotten, and it symbolizes a new beginning. Beside it may be placed Kreidolf's remaining picture-books which appeared in a long succession from 1898 onwards.

Development continued after the First World War. The Berlin publishing house of Cassirer (later to emigrate to England) began to take an interest in illustrated books and issued Christian Morgenstern's two volumes of children's poetry: *Das Hasenbuch* (1908) and *Klein Irmchen* (1921) with outstanding illustrations by K. F. Freyhold and J. L. Gampp. There was a child-like innocence about these picture-books which, properly speaking, should be the natural characteristic of the genre but which today is still found only infrequently. Such books, the idealistic productions of idealist publishers, writers, and illustrators, were to point the way until well into the thirties for artists like Eduard Bäumer, Tom Seidmann-Freud, Susanne Ehmcke,★ Marianne Scheel,★ Walter Bergmann, Beatrice Braun-Fock,★ and Conny Meissen. Other names might well be added to these, but all the books produced by these artists are difficult to track down today and instead of forming the foundation for a solid tradition, as occurred in England with books of a similar date, they have been allowed to go out of print and are often known only to collectors.

At about the same time there was developing a realistic style, with more of traditional painting about it, represented at its most masterly in the many books of Else Wenz-Vietor; while in the direction of refined romanticism there was the work of Elsa Eisgruber, whose pictures gave new life to many treasures of the German literary past. Yet another contrast appeared in the world portrayed by Walter Trier,★ whose down-to-earth drawings gave the clearest account of a period which was not exactly idyllic.

Although even the fascist régime did not stand in the way of the movement towards a revolutionary development in purely artistic matters, the cultural politics of national socialism showed a strong preference for sentimentality and an all-too-faithful representationalism. Anything stylized earned for itself very rapidly the label 'degenerate' and even if some artists were able to escape from the dangers of that time and themselves produce some very beautiful picture-books, there was no question of any further development. Then, with the coming of the war, a halt seemed to be called throughout Europe, while in the misery of the period immediately after the war, with its shattered cities and its tragic demoralization, the first strong and positive influences came from outside, especially from America. The revival which followed saw the recovery of what had been missed and the return to a characteristic home production, some proofs and examples of which may be discussed at this point.

A number of illustrations have been included of the current work of artists who were among the experimentalists of the thirties, such as Beatrice Braun-Fock (p. 113), Susanne Ehmcke (p. 196), and Marianne Scheel (p. 97), together with Walter Trier (p. 90) who was still alive and at work in

Marlene Reidel,
«Die Hexenuhr»,
München 1960

MORGENS FRÜH UM ACHT WIRD KAFFEE GEMACHT.

the first years after the war. Susanne Ehmcke★ is particularly interesting here since most of her books gain an enhanced unity of design from being both written and illustrated by the artist herself. Her style, which may today seem staid and rooted in tradition, represented at one time the start of a new clarity and gaiety in picture-books for the youngest children.

Katharina Maillard★ (p. 81), Johannes Grüger★ (p. 104), Johanna Rubin★ (p. 106), and Sigrid Heuck★ (p. 115) all have their roots in the traditions of the German picture-book, although they make use of new and to some extent highly effective graphic techniques. There is an interplay of markedly decorative styles with an almost copy-book naturalism and each artist has a strong individual gift for colour, largely finding expression in the use of opaque pastels or tempera. Sigrid Heuck and Katharina Maillard provide examples also of the use of montage, which gives their pictures a certain static tranquillity. This approach is complemented in the work of Johannes Grüger and Johanna Rubin by a use of line to enliven the text.

All four artists are seen at their best in picture-books for younger children at kindergarten level. At the same time, Grüger is a fine illustrator of Bible stories and shows a genuine feeling for children's rhymes in his illustrations for Christine Busta's beautiful volume of poetry, *Die Sternenmühle* (p. 104). Reinhard Herrmann★ is another artist who has taken a bold approach to Bible stories, working in a similar way with densely coloured surfaces in opaque, somewhat subdued tones (p. 156). He also makes an expressive use of heavy black lines. But the person who has brought real mastery to bear in the treatment of flat coloured surfaces is Marlene Reidel,★ working in a manner which has its origins in the lino-cut (p. 10). Her books, and especially the early ones which harked back to her own nursery, have a story-teller's colourful authenticity and power.

Two other outstanding picture-book artists, who are, however, also turning their talents to the needs of children who have already begun to read, are Gerhard Oberländer★ (p. 89) and Horst Lemke★ (p. 166). Oberländer can put his name to an extraordinarily rich and varied body of work in both colour and line and in recent years he has been concentrating chiefly on the illustration of fairy-tales.

With simple materials, sometimes only shreds of paper, Liselotte Schwartz★ has produced illustrations which have won for her a growing reputation, despite their restrained and ethereal manner. On the other hand, the graphic 'team' of Winter★ and Bischoff have made an opening for the techniques of modern advertising art in picture-books. This is a development which is welcome so long as it is carried out in a way as masterly as theirs, but the dangers of a method which relies so much upon decoration are obvious.

Reiner Zimnik★ has taken an entirely new direction with his picture-books, using the same pen both for drawing and writing and spontaneously elaborating his own very original ideas. From an international viewpoint his picture-stories, particularly those in black and white, are perhaps Germany's most individual contribution to the world of picture-books. There is also a marked strain of the moralist in Zimnik, holding as he frequently does a mirror up to the human species (p. 172). His most recent picture-books in colour are by no means so original as his earlier volumes in line only.

A naïvety in the interpretation of stories through pen-drawing is also to be found in the work of Janosch★ (p. 92) who has produced a quantity of picture-stories which look almost like sketch-books but which have great charm. There is a genuineness about the simplicity of his drawing which attests the directness of experience or of childhood memories. On the whole his work appeals more to grown-ups than to children, but this is not to deny that he has the talents to create good picture-books for children. He, too, has turned to colour work now with great success.

A certain naïvety of style—the sort of thing that is found in the work of many 'Sunday painters'—seems to be well suited to picture-books. The poetic realism of Georgy Stefula's★ *Paradies*, for instance (p. 151), is clearly heading in this direction, while the playful line drawing of Wanda Zacharias★ (p. 167) shows similar characteristics backed up by a delicate use of colour.

It is the drawings and pictures of Wiltrud Roser,★ however, which express at its purest the artist's sense of association with the child's experience. Without imitating the way children draw, her pictures nevertheless possess the same qualities (p. 83), and this perhaps explains her immediate success among children. Like Susanne Ehmcke she also writes her own stories. This genuine simplicity is also present in Heidrun Petrides' picture-book, *Der Xaver und der Wastl* (Zürich, Atlantis, 1962)[1] which is perhaps only to be expected, since the creator of both text and pictures was only fifteen years of age when she produced the book.

With the exception perhaps of Marianne Scheel,★ whose *Das Regenbogenhaus* draws all its life from colour, almost all the artists so far mentioned have their roots in graphic art. This would, therefore, seem to be the point to draw attention to Lilo Fromm★ who, although an outstanding draughtsman (see p. 13), has produced most of her children's books through a free use of paint. She is perhaps the most painterly of all Germany's picture-book artists even though it is scarcely possible to reproduce her brilliant palette in print.

Among the many other artists who should receive some mention here, there is only room for Kurth Wendtland, who is equally at home in the techniques of painting and of montage; Herbert Lentz, who captures so well for little children the dream-world of fantasy; Sofie Frenzel who excels at fairy-tale illustrations; and, finally, Günther Stiller and Wilfred Blecher, whose use of coloured crayon is introducing a new stylistic element into German picture-books.

For a long time it appeared as if the division of Germany would bring about two worlds whose books would differ more than the books of two quite separate nations. But today a lively exchange is taking place through several publishers, and the West is getting the opportunity to become familiar with the children's books of East Germany.

One of the first artists to claim attention in the West was Oleg Zinger★

---

[1] Translated as *Hans and Peter*. London, O.U.P., 1962; New York, Harcourt, Brace, 1963.

Lilo Fromm. *Das Kinderhaus* by Ingrid Bachér. Freiburg im Breisgau, Atlantis, 1965.

and the illustration given here (p. 73) is from one of the first picture-books to cross the frontier. Johanna Rubin★ (p. 106), whose outstanding graphic abilities have been so successful, is also from the East; and Werner Klemke★ (p. 87), equally well known on either side of 'the Curtain', is a teacher in the East Berlin Academy of Arts. These last two artists are a living proof of a powerful adherence to the old graphic traditions of Leipzig, where books were conceived as a complete unity of word and picture. Another example can be seen in Frans Haacken's★ interpretation of *Peter und der Wolf* (p. 92) which has as many champions in the West as in the East where it originated. We find here once again the powerful graphic use of black and white which, along with the type-face, gives the book a rare unity—even though the pervasive darkness of the pages may trouble some children.

The prevailing emphasis on forceful line-drawing is also present in the work of other highly regarded picture-book artists from East Germany, such as Hans Baltzer, Ingeborg Meyer-Rey, Eberhard Binder Stassfurth, and Erich Gürtzig.

Austria

As the centre of a widespread empire the Austria of the past naturally produced its own picture-books, ABCs and children's books for both information and enjoyment, even though it shared with its geographical neighbours a large part of the standard classics. With Germany it also shared something of the decline in book-illustration which set in towards the end of the nineteenth century, but at the beginning of the twentieth a fresh impulse sprang into being through the influence of the *Wiener Werkstätten*. Viennese educationists were also the first to recognize the important part played in education by children's own drawings.

The collapse of the monarchy brought about such a shrinkage in the market for Austrian children's books that impoverishment had to follow. This is only now being made up for by an intensive movement to spread worthwhile children's literature into all parts of the country.

Austria is able to point to a large production of picture-books aimed at a widespread public. The demand for expansion, however, inhibits experiment, for picture-books are in the best sense made to be enjoyed and are thus to a considerable extent conservative. There is no lack of colour or humour, as can be seen in such typical portrayals as the one opposite of little Stanislaus drawn by Romulus Candea. Susi Weigel's★ coloured picture-book, *Hannes und sein Bumpam*, is a good example of a worthwhile educational intention realizing itself in a popular style without compromising the need for good art (p. 141). Helga Aichinger's★ work is still modest in quantity, but promises a great deal. Her *Rattenfänger*, which won a prize at the Brussels World Fair, her illustrations for fairy stories and her cheap folding booklets all attract through a blend of lyrical and decorative elements. On the other hand, Wilhelm Jaruska★

14

(p. 68) represents the academic tradition, but with much vitality and expressiveness.

Promotion of and research into children's books are both being vigorously undertaken in Austria today and there can be little doubt that this will be reflected in new artistic developments.

Switzerland

Switzerland is another country whose picture-books of the past were shared with her neighbours. When one refers to the revitalization of the German-language picture-book around 1900 then it is to a Swiss, the former apprentice lithographer Ernst Kreidolf, that a decisive part must be credited, a fact which is not without influence in the later development of picture-books there.

Only after complete dissociation from her north-eastern neighbour in 1933 did Switzerland's production assume a strong national character. There then suddenly appeared such books as *Der Leuchtturm* (Zürich, 1936) by R. Schnitter, with illustrations by Berta Tappolet, the comical picture-stories by Elsa Möschlin, and the originally conceived drawings by Esther Hosch-Wackernagel for her stories about *Das lustige Männlein* (Basel, 1936).

In 1939 the artistic success of the Swiss National Fair strengthened the national consciousness. Later, during the war, many home-bred picture-books were produced and, soon after, there began to appear the fairy stories and other books illustrated by Hans Fischer,★ nicknamed Fis (pp. 160–1). Apart from these, which he often adapted or wrote himself, Hans Fischer was responsible for what are perhaps the finest illustrations for modern school textbooks.

Important influences have come from advertising and poster art, as seen, for instance, in Herbert Leupin's work and in books by Celestino Piatti★ (p. 67). Piatti has also produced some beautiful drawings for infants' school readers, and his famous owl-book now represents something of a milestone in modern picture-book art.

A sense of expansiveness coupled with the greatest pictorial charm characterizes all the work of the Grisons painter Alois Carigiet,★ and his *Schellen-Ursli* (p. 124) created a diminutive national figure who was to impress artists abroad as well as at home. This book appeared soon after the war when nothing of the same freshness or expressiveness was to be found in Germany. The rougher techniques of modern expressionism have found their way into picture-books in the works of such successful artists as Walter Grieder★ from Basel (p. 45).

The generously designed picture-books of Helen Kasser★ (p. 69) represent most clearly the Swiss connexion with the mainstream of modern European graphic art, while Lili Roth-Streiff★ embodies the tendency towards sweetness, towards a child's dream-world, which seems, alas, to be dying out, but which may be due for a revival (p. 82). Felix Hoffmann★ is assuredly the most versatile of these artists. His picture-book versions of fairy stories have become

world famous (p. 158) and his many pen-drawings and woodcuts can be found in all branches of literature and not just in children's books. Nevertheless, it is the fairy stories in particular which exemplify most beautifully his unparalleled ability to combine perfect craftsmanship with the delight of story-telling. Like many other artists he has also sought to measure his talents in a big illustrated volume of Bible stories.

Alongside such markedly stylized books as those by Helen Kasser, who has also illustrated books about animals for very young children, a place should be found for realistic books of information, especially those on topics connected with nature. The example in colour on p. 43 is from the work of Jörg Kühn,★ who, before his early death, was himself an almost professional zoologist and is beyond compare in the way that he is able to bring the life of the forest alive for children.

It might be thought self-evident that the Swiss national hero, William Tell, would be plentifully represented in books for children, but this is not entirely so. True, Otto Baumberger has converted Gotthelf's story of William Tell's son into pictures for older children and for adults, but it has been left to a young American woman to break the ground at picture-book level. Aliki's happy and colourful little story of William Tell and his son has by its very unconventional approach won for itself both praise and blame. Even less conventional is Warja Honegger-Lavater's★ fascinating attempt to present the subject by using a series of colourful symbols (p. 177). Paul Nussbaumer's★ *Der Knabe des Tell*, inspired by Gotthelf's story, abides much more closely by accepted standards (p. 47) and tells the tale with simple feeling and with great delight in colour. It is a good example of the way in which elements from popular tradition may be combined with the expressive possibilities of modern graphic techniques.

Vladimir Bobri, «The March Wind», New York 1957

Picture-Books in America

It may seem odd that to many people 'comics, cowboys, and chewing-gum' stand as symbols for a nation which saved part of the world from starvation after the Second World War. By this act, however, America won for herself a right to have some say in the programme for re-education in the defeated territories, and along with other allies, she certainly had a considerable influence on what was read or not read in Germany during the years immediately after the war.

Now what could America offer to children apart from the three well-known c's that have already been mentioned? What about the strip-cartoons, whose wretchedly halting dialogue proceeded from the characters' mouths in balloons all too closely resembling those produced by bubble-gum? Were these not a natural concomitant of American troops and American produce? Did they not, in fact, destroy the small amount of good that was still to be found in a war-wasted continent? These questions have been asked frequently and reproachfully and in many developing countries they are still being asked today. In her defence, however, it must be said that America herself was least happy about her questionable monopoly which was responsible for spreading so much ribaldry and so much bad taste and which had begun long before with the 're-education' programme in her own nurseries and schoolrooms.

On the other hand, post-war America had a number of likeable emissaries which should also be considered. There was, for instance, the children's book which appeared in Germany very shortly after the war (although first published in America in 1937) whose text, by Munro Leaf, surely held as much significance as Robert Lawson's illustrations. This was *Ferdinand*, the story of the bull who will not fight, a book which set peaceful attitudes and the enjoyment of life above conventional heroism. Munro Leaf himself later took to drawing and he has written and illustrated a number of semi-didactic but always enjoyable picture-stories which have brought ideals of international unity to children all over the world. They have been as quickly understood by the village children of India as by those of the American prairie.

The second character who, even more markedly than Ferdinand, became an image for European children was 'the happy lion' of Louise Fatio and Roger Duvoisin* (p. 71)—a similarly pacific hero who did away with the idea that only the violent could be fit examples for children. Both of these figures were surely the spiritual heirs of Babar, king of the elephants, who very early in his career travelled across from France to America.

Over and above this, however, what was it that made American picture-books such an important factor in post-war education? Because of his addiction to communication through pictures the American allots an important role to visual considerations as an aid to education and instruction. The important publishers of children's books possess very skilful readers and editors with a great sense of responsibility. They are past masters in the recognition of new talent and in the careful combination of words and pictures so that the right authors are brought together with the right illustrators.

Standards are continuously maintained through a critical press, through specialist journals and surveys, and through an outstanding system of children's libraries served by professionally trained staff. Such awards as the Caldecott Medal, presented annually for the year's most distinguished picture-book, also contribute a lot to the general raising of quality. All this, however, would be useless if the American publishers did not have at their disposal an enormous number of fine artists who are determined to give of their best in their work for children. This pool of artists was, and still is, replenished with a steady stream of immigrants: Russians, Poles, Scandinavians, Italians, Germans, and even Greeks, Dutchmen, Swiss, and Mexicans, who bring an exotic strangeness to America's multifarious other qualities. Often their names will return in triumph to their native lands on the covers of their books—and there are even some artists, like the typically French Françoise★ (p. 126) or the Italian Munari★ (p. 61), who have become American authors without leaving their own countries. Or think of Roger Duvoisin,★ the writer and illustrator of dozens of successful picture-books. His Swiss homeland, which he left at the age of thirty, could never have offered him such opportunities for development.

America also provides examples of every style of illustration, from the exactness in representation of nature of a Rojankovsky★ (p. 98) to the poetic impressionism of a Maurice Sendak★ (as in *Charlotte and the white horse*, p. 84), and to the work of Helen Borten★ (pp. 136 and 178) or Ann and Paul Rand★ (p. 179) whose experiments tend strongly towards the abstract (almost forming a guide to education in art). With Leo Lionni's *Little blue and little yellow* (New York, McDowell, 1959; Leicester, Brockhampton, 1962) America has even produced the first attempt at a completely abstract picture-book which has gained any sort of popularity. Since an illustration without colour would tell you nothing at all, none has been included but this book certainly represents an interesting stage in the history of picture-books.

It would be wrong not to mention here the two famous couples Alice and Martin Provensen★ (p. 102) and Ingri and Edgar Parin d'Aulaire★ (p. 192) who created a new type of picture-book in their big, semi-informational albums. The latter display both courage and a dash of naïvety in their approach to some of the great subjects of history and literature.

Instruction, in one way or another, is also the main concern of a number of other author-illustrators such as the husband and wife team Berta and Elma Hader★ (p. 193) or the irrepressible Dr. Seuss. Writing under this name or another pseudonym (Theo Le Sieg) the real Theodore Geisel has produced a number of picture-books which conceal their educational intentions behind grotesque illustrations and knockabout play with words.

The double talent for conceiving and writing stories and then illustrating them, is one which has been noted previously as tending to give such books a special degree of unity. Among the other artists who can be singled out in this

Roger Duvoisin, «White Snow, Bright Snow», New York 1947

category are Karla Kuskin* (pp. 114 and 153) and Marie Hall Ets, who has produced a group of delightfully good-humoured picture-books rather unexpectedly illustrated in black and white. Aliki Brandenberg, who was mentioned in the last chapter, and Tomi Ungerer* are artist-story-tellers who have settled down in America. Aliki came originally from Greece and Ungerer from Alsace, and although he has gained standing very rapidly in the U.S.A. as a cartoonist, Ungerer's most famous book, *The three robbers*, was in fact first published in Germany.

The subject of Red Indians, until recently somewhat neglected, has attracted an astonishing number of picture-books (pp. 136, 137, and 193). Apart from these examples, special mention should also be made of Velino Herrara's magnificent illustrations for Ann Clark's *In my mother's house* (New York, Viking, 1941) and J. Brewer McGaw's *Little Elk hunts buffalo* (New York, Nelson, 1961), a picture-book about Indian sign-language.

The mingling of American and foreign styles can be seen in the work of such artists as the American-Japanese Taro Yashima in books like *Umbrella* and *The village tree* (Viking), or the Mexican Antonio Frasconi* (p. 116), whose expressive illustrations have introduced entirely new elements into the art of the picture-book. The same thing could be said of Jacqueline Ayer,* whose transparent and delicately drawn pictures bring home to children something of the land of Thailand (p. 133). Some of the less well-known work of Ezra Jack Keats* is also concerned with subjects set in the Far East, but he has shown himself more sympathetic to the everyday life of his own country, especially in his beautifully observed picture-books about the small boy Peter.

Despite modern artistic developments, there are still plenty of admirable picture-books appearing in an almost academic style which one is tempted to call 'the new realism'. Proof of this can be seen in the work of such versatile picture-book artists as Leonard Weisgard* (p. 149), Barbara Cooney* (p. 148), Marc Simont* (pp. 64 and 142), and Garth Williams* (p. 65).

It is striking how readily American picture-book artists have turned to traditional themes in exploiting the sureness of their technical accomplishments. Marcia Brown* has devoted enormous graphic skill to producing her very individual versions of such tales as *Cinderella* and *Once a mouse*—the books for which she achieved the distinction of being twice awarded the Caldecott Medal. Less versatile, but equally consistent, Adrienne Adams* has shown a similar skill in her use of colour lithography.

Paul Galdone* is notable for his completely successful interpretation of the humour of nursery tales and rhymes (as well as his bold re-illustrations of Edward Lear). His colour drawings match the atmosphere of his subjects and contrast with the much more consciously modern graphic work of Margot Zemach in her illustrations to traditional folk-tales.

It has not been possible to show more recent illustrators such as Ed Emberley, Evaline Ness, Dahlov Ipcar, Ed Young, Anne Rockwell and Eric Carle, but this is to some extent an indication of the way in which the United States incorporates within its boundaries the multifarious activity that would normally be found in a whole continent.

Scandinavia and the Netherlands

As we shall see later with England, many Scandinavian picture-book artists like to be given a story to illustrate. In other words, the text, however short, carries a comparable importance to the pictures. Scandinavia scarcely knows the kind of picture-book found in German-speaking countries and occasionally in America, where the book is conceived in visual terms and the text is often supplied by the illustrator himself.

So important is the text that it may even predominate in such a delightful alphabet book as Britt Hallqvist's (p. 38) where the illustrator, Stig Lindberg,★ has woven his pictures around the words. In most cases, as far as it is possible to judge, the text and pictures possess a similar quality and match each other excellently. For instance, in Astrid Lindgren's *Tomte Tummeltott* (*The Tomten*. London, Constable; New York, Coward, 1961) the ethereal poetry of the story is reflected in Harald Wiberg's atmospheric illustrations done in watercolour in a traditional style.

Scandinavian children tend to be deluged with enjoyable books, with colourful books, with witty books. The most famous of these is Larsson's *Ett hem* (*At home*) which is perhaps better described as a household rather than a children's book. It first appeared at the beginning of this century (Stockholm, 1904) and found its way into all parts of Europe, taking with it a sense of humour and a feeling for sunshine which have never since disappeared from the books of these northern lands. Who will say that Scandinavian children are not somewhat indemnified for those long winters with all that snow, for so little sunshine and for their reputed tendency towards melancholia.

Sweden

The Swedish tradition in book illustration is dominated by Elsa Beskow who, for more than half a century, worked in so many ways to establish a style for her country. Her most devoted follower, especially in books at kindergarten level, has been Eva Billow who has several times won awards for her work. Among the other notable picture-book artists perhaps the best known outside Sweden is Inga Borg, who found fame with her reindeer book *Parrak* (London and New York, Warne, 1959) and has followed it with several other picture-books about animals. Harald Wiberg and Ilon Wikland★ have also gained an international audience through their illustrations for Astrid Lindgren's books, but two other artists are less well known: Ingrid vang Nyman, who caught so well the character of famous Pippi Longstocking, and Lasse Sandberg, whose pictures retain better than most Astrid Lindgren's typically Swedish sense of humour. Lasse Sandberg has also recently produced some big picture-books of her own.

Among the artists chosen for the following anthology there are Stig Lindberg★ (p. 38), one of Sweden's most productive illustrators; Helga Henschen★ (p. 97), the brilliant illustrator of Britt Hallqvist's *Festen i Hulabo*, a book of poems which won the Nils Holgersson Medal; Poul Strøyer★ (p. 111), whose amusing stories are beginning to find their way into translations; Ulf Löfgren★ (p. 140) for his particularly original picture-book, *Barnen i Djungeln*; and Elisabeth Landen★ (p. 152), the illustrator of a series of Bible stories in verse.

Finland

Both Finland and Norway seem to me to be especially rich in sonorous children's poetry, which is capable of conveying impressions even to those who have not mastered those notoriously complex languages. The colourful word-play of this poetry has inspired a number of artists to match it with exquisite illustrations, as in the series of books from Finland, *Lasten Kultainen Kalevala*, with pictures by Tapio Tapiovaara, Maija Karma, Helga Sjöstedt, and Heljä Lahtinen. These are only little books, illustrated simply and with few colours, but they offer the child a variegated world in poetry, beautifully complemented by the pictures. Maija-Kaarina Nenonen seems to me to be another artist who has caught the spirit of these northern lands in her illustrations to the lovely picture-book *Prinsessa Sinisilma*.

Drawing by Ilon Wikland.

All these Finnish books have been published by Werner Söderström whose enterprise is quite astonishing considering the smallness and sparseness of the country. He is also the publisher of Tove Jansson, Finland's most famous author-illustrator of children's books, for all that she writes in Swedish. Her work unites within itself a world of Nordic intricacy, Scandinavian humour, and a happy gift for the expressive use of line-drawing. The illustration on p. 168 is the more amusing for our knowledge that Tove Jansson likes to prepare her stories during the summer months, spent in the isolation of a Baltic island.

Norway

Like the Finns, the Norwegians can point to a rich choice of children's poetry, much of it superbly illustrated. Their famous story-teller, poet and artist—Thorbjörn Egner—is, of course, known in many countries, but interesting work is also being done by Mette Borchgrevink, who uses paint in an original way, and Reidar Johan Berle, an illustrator of animal fables. Paul Gauguin★ (p. 95) has a special talent for expressing in pictures the nonsense elements in children's poetry.

Denmark

Denmark, the smallest of these northern countries, has perhaps the most fruitful output of picture-books. One of her most sensitive artists is Ib Spang-Olsen★ and a coloured drawing of his is reproduced opposite (p. 25). Two Danish picture-stories which have gained a reputation as classics are also represented: Jens Sigsgaard's *Palle alene i Verden*, with illustrations by Arne Ungermann★ (p. 144), and Aáge Gitz-Johansen's★ *Gaba, den lille Grønlaender* (p. 135). Attention should also be drawn to Egon Mathiesen,★ whose boldly simplified drawings for *Mis med de blå Øjne* (p. 63) caused a considerable stir of excitement and pleasure. His book *Aben Osvald* (Copenhagen, Gyldendal, 1947) is one of the wittiest examples of the comic animal story.

The Netherlands

Similarities of language (Finland excepted) allow for a certain amount of literary interchange among the countries of Scandinavia—an advantage which is not so easily enjoyed by the Netherlands. Nevertheless, children's books in this country have a long and colourful history, beautifully exemplified by

24

Ib Spang-Olsen, «Abrikosia», København 1958

Leonard de Vries in his anthology of facsimiles *Bloempjes der vreugd* (Amsterdam, De Bezige, 1958).[1] If the Netherlands can no longer compete so easily in the struggle for more books in colour, then this is partly due to the problems inherent in printing for a very small market.

As in Scandinavia, the illustration of poetry and nursery rhymes has always been important. The example here from Marijke Doornekamp's★ *Oude Rijmpjes* (p. 94) seems to me to be a model of good book design for children, full of kindness and good humour. A similarly amusing book of verses is the little volume *Versjes die wy nooit vergeten*, illustrated by Max Velthuijs (The Hague, Van Goor, 1962).

Dick Bruna,★ literally, presents quite a different picture (p. 179). The many little books that he has created have broken new ground in the way that they portray the everyday world of the young child with their bold drawing and their bright, flat colours. John Toorenbeek's illustrations for *Mijn eerste book over God* (Utrecht, Chantecleer, 1959) and for several animal books have a similar kind of simplicity. Both of these artists are far removed in style from Jaap Tol, whose recent illustrations to two books by Frans van Anrooy presage the emergence of a new and very individual talent in European picture-books.

[1] Leonard de Vries has organized a book on very similar lines for early English children's books, translating even his Dutch title into *Flowers of delight* (London, Dobson, 1965). His examples have been drawn from specimens in the Osborne Collection of Early Children's Books at Toronto.

Picture-Books in England

Children's book illustration in Great Britain has almost as distinguished a tradition as that of children's literature, and it is significant for the modern picture-book that much of the work of artists like Randolph Caldecott, Kate Greenaway, and Beatrix Potter has remained in print to the present time. For the public attitude to picture-books is subject to an unwitting conservatism. What was enjoyed by one generation is automatically held to be enjoyable for its offspring, and although this may be understandable it can also be inhibiting for new artists with new ideas.

For this reason many modern picture-books in England adhere to a conventional, narrative style in pictorial representation, owing little to new developments in graphic processes or to fashions in the adult world of art or advertising. The foremost representative of this traditional approach is undoubtedly Edward Ardizzone* (p. 112) whose prolific output is founded on a complete mastery of the associated techniques of pen-drawing and water-colour. The *Tim* books are his most characteristic as well as his most famous children's books, and exemplify not only his individual style and his feeling for places, buildings, and ships but also his subsidiary, but equally attractive, abilities as a story-teller.

A very similar approach to pictorial representation is that of 'Bettina,'* the pen-name of Bettina Ehrlich. She is an Austrian by birth and her stories are set almost without exception in a Mediterranean environment which gives them a rather exotic, holiday flavour. Her free use of line has a marked similarity to that of Ludwig Bemelmans, who was born in the same quarter of South-east Europe as herself (pp. 138 and 139).

Another artist whose best work is almost inseparable from her own stories is Violet Drummond* (p. 171). Her reliance on pen-drawing and water-colour relates her style to that of Bettina and Ardizzone, but much of her drawing lies closer to caricature and is entirely in keeping with the comic invention of her stories. William Papas,* a cartoonist by profession, has shown how the technique can be successfully adapted to picture-books. His square-format children's books in colour and monochrome have brought a fresh vigour and wit to the traditional style. Antony Maitland* (p. 173), too, has produced a number of pleasantly coloured picture-books, but his most successful work has been done in line for the illustration of children's fiction.

As soon as one turns to the work of the less traditional graphic artists in English picture-books, one is aware of the emergence of a more cosmopolitan style. This is related to the development of offset lithography in European children's books during the 1930s and it is no coincidence that Puffin Picture Books (p. 185) owed their inception to examples of cheap factual books from

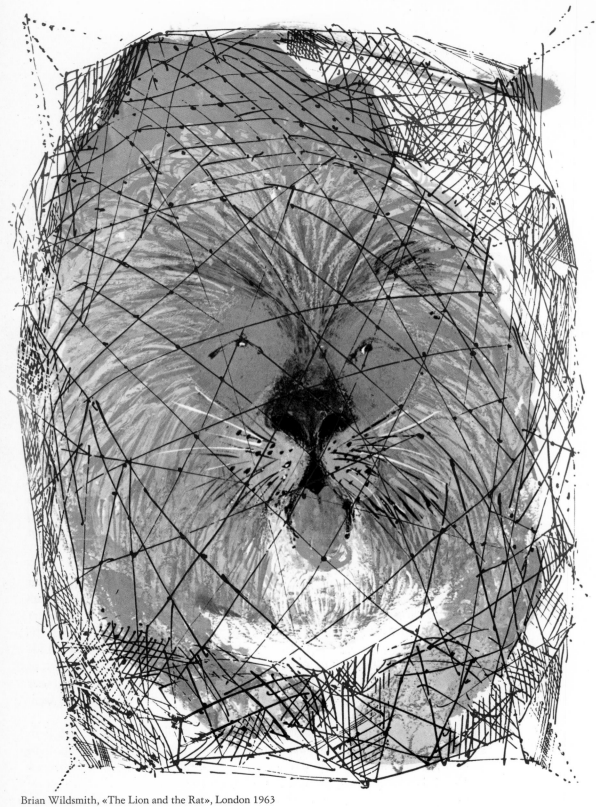

Brian Wildsmith, «The Lion and the Rat», London 1963

Russia and the early Père Castor books from France. The Puffin series was to encourage some of the best graphic work ever to appear in English children's books, and artists such as Paxton Chadwick,★ Eileen Mayo,★ Clarke Hutton, and Phyllis Ladyman have since made a notable contribution to picture-books from other publishers. Puffins were probably the inspiration for the *Pleiades Books* which appeared after the Second World War, edited by Oliver Hill★ and Hans Tisdall★ (p. 184). As bound books with an educational purpose these were a decade ahead of their time and have unfortunately long been out of print.

Kathleen Hale,★ an early contributor to Puffins, was one of the first picture-book artists to score a success with new techniques in lithography with her big books about Orlando the Marmalade Cat (p. 110). But at about the same time the international flavour of English picture-books was increased with the appearance of the books of two immigrant Poles who teamed up under the name of Lewitt-Him.★ They brought a fresh eye to the colour and design of their gay stories, of which only *The Little Red Engine gets a Name*[1] is still in print (p. 186).

Since the 1950s the 'modern' style has developed through the work of a number of artists who have been closely connected with advertising or with the teaching of graphic processes. One of the key figures here is William Stobbs,★ who combines mastery of line with an ability to organize colour in carefully designed page openings. He has caught the simplicity needed in books for small children in some of his illustrations to folk-tales (p. 80), while in his elaborate illustrations to Chekhov's short story *Kashtanka* he showed a gift for more sophisticated work without losing his feeling for what children like. A similarly attractive use of colour and line is found in the books of Alan Howard★ (pp. 33 and 78), whose first picture-book preceded *Kashtanka* by eight years and was based on another Russian source—*Peter and the Wolf*, a theme of international appeal to illustrators.

In the work of such artists as Gerald Rose★ and John Burningham★ the possibilities of painting have been explored to an extent which makes it unfortunate that the examples of their work here could not be given in colour (pp. 72 and 108). Both artists have a boldly original approach to form and colour, coupled with a rich sense of the comic and the grotesque particularly appealing to young children.

Many of the artists mentioned in this chapter have received the British Library Association's award of the Kate Greenaway Medal, but none has achieved quite the same degree of acclamation as the 1962 winner, Brian Wildsmith.★ Although he was an experienced illustrator in line before this date, his emergence as a colourist, first with *The Arabian Nights* and then with his *ABC*, was quite spectacular. His success has been confirmed in his series of large format versions of some of La Fontaine's fables and in his more recent pictorial studies of birds and animals. These books are almost entirely visual—a

[1] Leslie Wood has since continued the illustration of the Little Red Engine books in an entirely appropriate style. Among other vehicles which have trundled along behind, perhaps the most notable are those such as *The Little Train* (Parrish, 1946) and *The Little Horse-Bus* (Parrish, 1952; New York, Lothrop, 1954) which Dorothy Craigie drew in collaboration with their distinguished author, Graham Greene.

William Papas. *No Mules*. London, O.U.P., 1967.

characteristic even more pronounced in his controversial *123* which replaces the conventional number book with a play of almost abstract forms which sparkle and glow like stained-glass windows.

Like Stobbs and Wildsmith, a number of other artists have turned to picture-books after first gaining a reputation as illustrators in line. Charles Keeping,★ for instance, was responsible for a great deal of strongly individual work in monochrome before producing his recent group of intensely coloured and equally individual picture-stories about children and animals. Raymond Briggs★ and Victor Ambrus★ have also followed up their success as line illustrators with some fine colour work, the former particularly in his carefully chosen small collections of nursery rhymes, the latter in his illustrations to factual books and hero tales and in his adaptations of Hungarian folk-tales. Recent picture-books by such illustrators as Gaynor Chapman, Gareth Floyd, and Barry Wilkinson bear further witness to the success that can be achieved by artists who are first schooled in the disciplines of line or monochrome illustration.

Mediterranean Picture-Books

Spain   North and central Europeans are not inclined to credit Spain with any picture-book literature of her own. Typical productions are those cheap and garishly sentimental wares whose covers and pages are cut out to the shape of the book's main character. Furthermore, if this happens to be a princess, then she will have a real little necklace on, or if a policeman, then he will have a whistle which actually whistles. A Spanish farm-girl will have a little jar of honey dangling from her cardboard wrist, or a Chinese boy a real chopstick. Books like this for the youngest age group are found everywhere and are of the most variable quality. It can be quite surprising to discover inside their commercialized and clamorous covers pages of pictures which are very attractive and which children may well find both amusing and instructive, as, for instance, the series about children from different parts of the world, describing little Negroes, Eskimoes, Arabs, and Indians and their way of life. The better-quality books of this kind are even on the shelves of children's public libraries, but, one suspects, for much the same reason that the carrot was hung in front of the donkey.

Apart from this industry, whose products range from the brash to the sugary, and are often completely worthless, there is a growing quantity of picture-books in the modern style, designed to give pleasure and even more important, information to children who have just learned to read. There are fewer of these books than in, say, Germany or England, but publishers such as Aguilar, Doncel, Juventud, and others are making tremendous efforts to improve the situation. French influences—from such series as the *Albums du Père Castor*—predominate, beautifully revitalized and changed in form; but Spain has not really made any distinctive contribution of her own in the present development of picture-books. Even in books which are technically very good, the round-eyed, doll-like faces of the children often betray the influence of comics or film cartoons, and the careful production and wide distribution of educational books like encyclopaedias is still no substitute for a native tradition.

I do not know how far or how vital the influence continues to be of those broadsheets known as *Aleluyas*, which have played such an important part in providing amusement for Spanish children in the past. The relationship between broadsides and comics and picture-books is difficult enough to disentangle at the best of times even in one's own country. Spain's most notable contribution to the world of picture-books lies in a quite different direction, and stems from the fact that Spanish children, like so many in southern climates, mature earlier and thus make a start in reading literature at an age when many of our children are still looking at picture-books with quite simple texts. It is for this reason (which, in fact, applies largely to France as well) that such literature is often provided for Spanish children in editions illustrated by the country's best illustrators. Such writers as Federico Garcia Lorca, Juan Ramon Jiménez, Rafael Morales, Luis Rosales, and Miguel de Unamuno have written not only stories but also plays and poems for young people, and it is alongside such work, or else in the field of such school subjects as history, geography, or science at an upper level, that Spain's most characteristic and striking illustrative work is to be found. It may be argued that these books are intended for a higher age group than those previously dealt with here—but through their use of colour and their format they take on much of the character of picture-books.

The examples which have been selected demonstrate various trends, for instance, Munoa's★ colour-drawing for Jiménez's beautiful *Platero y yo* (p. 36), which matches in a masterly way the quality of the text, uniting delicacy and warmth with intellectual grasp. A typical illustration by Perellón for a children's book by I. M. Sanchez-Silva is also shown (p. 131). Careful observation is here gently exaggerated to form a completely satisfying picture entirely characteristic of the Spanish approach.

The illustration to the book of Mexican legends (p. 191) is just one example from the many books on history or culture which succeed in bringing the past alive for children of all ages. The illustrator, Lorenzo Goñi★ (also represented on p. 37), has perhaps the fullest range of ability at his command, although he is a self-taught artist who has been deaf since childhood. As the chief illustrator of Sanchez-Silva's books, and especially *Marcellino pan y vino*, his reputation has spread beyond his own country, but he has in fact illustrated a great number of books, including many for young children. For an artist with such a delicate and precise style in drawing he shows a remarkable response to the possibilities of using bold colour in his illustrations.

On the whole, Spanish book illustration is undergoing some interesting developments, both in picture-books and in children's books using illustrations to supplement the text. People are occupying themselves, even at the theoretical level, with the educational problems arising from all this, and those artists willing to give their best for children are being faced with a much more engrossing situation than formerly. Several young artists of great promise have recently taken up the challenge of picture-books for the youngest children, so that altogether a lively future looks to be in store.

Italy

Spain and France both provide examples of crudely popular picture-books for young children giving way gradually to a more elevated modern style where text and pictures are planned in much greater harmony. Italy is very similar. She had little in the way of a picture-book tradition until, after the war, there in disgrace. Far from it; very far from it! He was famous and clever and much more talked about than ever Freda Pigeon had been.

Purring with pleasure, he crept from behind the red parcels trolley and, although stiff in his joints and nipped with cold, set off at a trot for Mulberry's, the big store in the High Street. No doubt the manageress of the staff-canteen had put out a tasty fish supper for him. She would be disappointed if he failed to lap it up.

It was still hardly light when Limping Ginger snuggled

Alan Howard, «Limping Ginger of London Town», London 1962

appeared the novelty books of Bruno Munari.★ These were the work of an extraordinarily gifted artist (p. 61), but today his picture-books lack much of his old inventiveness and are indeed to be found only in America. Beyond this, the delightful series of picture-books on fairy-tale subjects by Ugo Fontana★ deserves a mention—exemplified by the picture opposite from Laura Draghi's fine book on 'the guardian angel'. Nicolo Simbari's *Gennarino* (New York, J. B. Lippincott; London, O.U.P., 1962) was a colourful book of great promise which has so far had no successor. Indeed, the strength of the modern Italian picture-book, as with that of Spain, lies in its literary, not to say satiric contribution which presupposes the earlier maturation of Italian children as well as their visual education through television and stories in pictures.

The boldest work represented here is that of Luzzati★ (p. 49), whose preference is for legendary or fairy-story subjects which he paints in a free style reminiscent of Rouault. There is no better example of the way modern painting has impinged upon picture-books. Giulio Cingoli's and Giancarlo Carloni's★ illustrations for the famous *Il fagiano Gaetano* (p. 77) similarly stand out as the possible opening of a new way for picture-books. This story of a chase combines qualities which are child-like and at the same time almost philosophical, and its illustrations—the expression of an age deeply conscious of symbols—balance the text in a way which will suit both children and adults. Ennio di Majo's★ illustrations (p. 91) are likewise not entirely free from irony, but they are likely to appeal more strongly to young children.

Gianni Rodari is a well-known writer from the camp of the left-wing intellectuals, but one who is well able to combine biting satire with a simple style and a most innocent poetry. His books have proved extraordinarily inspiring to illustrators and the example (p. 123)—again by Giancarlo Carloni —depicts a highly topical theme and one which here occasioned some almost frightening illustrations—but typical of present trends in Italy for all that.

Even though all these examples may point to a high achievement in graphic art, the refinements of this pictorial manner which supplements the text so amazingly well are only perhaps capable of being fully understood in a country where pictorial symbols are accessible to children from their earliest years in the form of films, television, and picture stories in magazines. It remains to be seen if this achievement has been gained at the cost of reading.

Greece

As a poor country, Greece has only a tiny market for books and her publishing activity is consequently limited. Fairy stories and nursery rhymes predominate among the books for young children, but they include all kinds of strongly appealing publications, particularly from the point of view of texts. The cost

Ugo Fontana. *Storie dell' Angelo Custode* by Laura Draghi. Florence, Vallecchi, 1959.

Rafael Munoa, «Platero y yo», Madrid 1963

of printing is a sufficient reason against there being very many picture-books in colour, and the example here (p. 101) is by Louisa Montesantou,★ who, although educated abroad, has rendered great services to children's books in Greece.

Illustration by L. Goñi.

Öö

ÖVERSTEN är van vid lydnad.
Han är regementets prydnad.
Stjärnströdd är hans axelklaff.
När han ryter blir man paff.

Stig Lindberg, «A B C», Stockholm 1953

Israel

In Israel there have been, and still are, so many other problems to be solved that the question of picture-books has not received attention to the same extent as in northern countries. Except for folk-tales Israel has no traditional material on hand, but writers and artists from all over the world have come into the country with their various ideas, styles, talents, and there is the possibility of a rich and diverse future. So far, however, no common denominator has been found. Conventional, not to say old-fashioned, illustrations stand side by side with advanced, boldly modern ones—although the latter are for the present still in the minority.

The two examples selected here are from picture-books of quite different types. The one showing a child reading (p. 146) comes from a cheap little booklet which typifies the kind of reading matter found in any kibbutz, with the daily life of the community depicted plainly in verse and pictures. It was published more than fifteen years ago, whereas the second example (p. 107) is much more recent, and is a superb production carried out with one eye on the international picture-book market. It is a witty animal fable and may well signify the start of a true Israeli style in picture-books.

I should have liked to round off this section with a consideration of picture-books in Turkey, Egypt, and the lands of North Africa. Much of the material which was available, however, proved to be either indifferent in quality and character or else tendentious—the politically biased material from Egypt above all. Nevertheless, a great deal is happening in these countries and the next few years could see many changes, provided that political stability can be achieved.

Picture-Books in France

Any history of picture-books since the First World War must assign a place of honour to France. First and foremost there is the painter Jean de Brunhoff, creator of the six great Babar books which have already achieved the rank of classics. Even the changes in format and in the niceties of colour-work (such as *Struwwelpeter* suffered a hundred years earlier), while they offend against the perfection of the original editions, do not detract in any way from the popularity of the books.

Again, there are the picture-books of Samivel whose artistry has turned them into collectors' pieces. Such books as *Bon voyage, Monsieur Dumollet* (Paris, Delagrave, 1942) and *Les malheurs d'Ysengrin* (Paris, Delagrave, 1939) may not be familiar to French children today, but by their taste and their refined wit they stand witness to the traditions of France. Or there are the *Albums du Père Castor* which, through their publisher and his chief illustrator, Rojankovsky, revolutionized the pictorial treatment of factual material in the nineteen-thirties. Today these books are something of an institution, serving the needs of children and their teachers as well as ever, but no longer showing the same impulse towards new methods of presentation. From time to time an artist of some consequence will find his way into the series, such as Paul-Emile Victor★ (p. 129), whose representations of fact retain both wit and a strong sense of narrative. Even bolder is the book *La montagne du souriceau*,

Marlenka Stupica. *Labodi* by Marcel Aymé. Ljubljana, Mladinska, 1963.

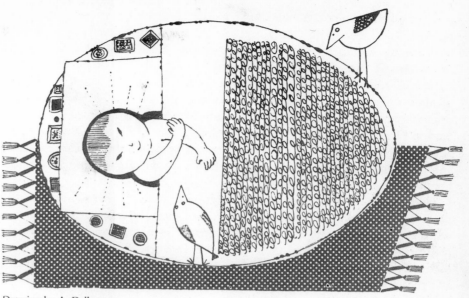

Drawing by A. Delhumeau.

illustrated by René Moreu★ (p. 195), to whom we owe a variety of interesting books. The volume *Quand Coulicoco dort*, illustrated by Kersti Chaplet (Paris, Flammarion, 1964), could be added to these examples to show that the traditions of the Père Castor series are still alive and that both information and a modern graphic approach can be combined within the covers of a cheap and unpretentious little book.

It seems remarkable that an outstanding artist like Colette Portal should have had her first book published in Germany (*Das Leben einer Königin*, p. 86) for it belongs among the most attractive and characteristic of contemporary French picture-books. Since 1962, however, this young artist has gained recognition in her own country and in America and England.

The publishers Hatier are bringing out a series of very imposing and decorative picture-books, which may be to some extent aimed at the international market, but which seem to me to be thoroughly typical of the current French taste for a combination of sweetness with modern and expensive production. Two examples here are Pascal Claude-Lafontaine's★ *La fille au sourire* (p. 134), a book of delicate and beautifully atmospheric graphic quality, and Micheline Chevallier's★ *Yo, le petit Tibétain* (p. 132), whose exotic and decorative charm leads us into a quite alien world. Other titles in this series are Napoli's *Aventure au Mont-Saint-Michel* (1963), a book whose strange atmosphere cannot be conveyed through any single example; Monica and François Régis Bastide's *Joachim quelque chose* (1959) and Micheline Maurel's *Contes d'agate*, illustrated by Annick Delhumeau (1960; see above).

Outsiders find it puzzling that a French illustrator like Françoise,★ who was so completely steeped in French subjects (p. 126), should, as an artist, have been so obviously at home in America. Her picture-books, despite their apparent simplicity, have a peculiarly sensitive feeling for rural France.

One of the most interesting contributions of present-day France to the modern picture-book is to be found in the cheap series of religious books published by Éditions du Cerf (pp. 152, 154, and 155). There is a completely fresh impulse behind the work of these artists: Alain le Foll,★ who has also made some exciting cut-out books, and who here attacks the hackneyed subject of Noah in a very unconventional way; Jacques le Scanff,★ who has brought an impressively simple sensibility not only to *Jonas* but also to several other Bible stories; and finally Jean Jacouton★ who has portrayed David and Saul as Orientals to the tips of their sandals. There is a freshness about these attempts which is reminiscent of the Père Castor studio thirty years earlier— and through their very cheapness these books should find a wide circulation for themselves.

There is, on the whole, an astonishingly rich fund of worthwhile picture-books available to French children. It is said of them, however, that, at an age when our children still have their noses buried in picture-books, they are already reading the classics of their literature. But here, too (and especially in the field of information books), there is a change taking place so that pictures, and therefore picture-books too, are increasingly being brought into use in teaching the younger age groups. Picture-books introduce children, above all, to such topics as nature and the countryside and life in distant lands. Like Spain and Italy, France knows all too well those sumptuously illustrated books with extensive texts which bear an outward resemblance to the traditional picture-books of the past but which are really aimed at older children.

Jörg Kühn, «Der Wald und seine Tiere», Zürich 1963

Picture-Books from Eastern Europe

If I group East European picture-books into one section of this Introduction it is by no means because I consider them all much of a sameness. As a rule, however, one is compelled to think of them in similar terms since they reach us from a world which is not always freely accessible and about which our information comes through more or less official channels or from confidential sources. As a rule it is not very easy for us to go into a bookshop in Prague or Warsaw and automatically get our bearings on the present state of children's books in those places. Even if we could we should receive a completely false impression, since we should see only a tiny part of the wealth of Polish or Czechoslovakian picture-books, most of which go out of print soon after publication. Such occasions as the International Book Fair at Frankfurt and the Children's Book Fair at Bologna provide some opportunity for orientation but the only objective way would be to journey as an observer, interviewing children, booksellers, parents, artists, and then, all over again, children.

Russia

Russia stands out from the other countries. A thoroughgoing realism is predominant there of the kind which we in the West are familiar with chiefly in factual books. Lebedev,* whose books have been widely distributed, is a pioneer in this, although he is also able to show some work in a much freer vein. The realist manner must avoid dullness at all costs and can in fact possess both vigour and a delicate poetry (pp. 79 and 127). There is also some tendency towards a greater stylization, but this is found much less often.

What is really surprising about all this is that at the beginning of the twenties Russia was prominent as the country which created the prototype of the cheap modern picture-book. The greatest stylistic freedom predominated and the Russian example influenced Western Europe. Clearly, however, those concerned with the state-direction of culture were of the opinion that all these different developments in style were not designed to win over to books the great mass of new consumers—the newly literate. Nevertheless, here as elsewhere, it is understood that a development towards greater latitude in artistic matters is gradually taking place.

Besides Vladimir Lebedev, mention should be made of Yuri Y. Vasnetsov (p. 79) and Tatjana Mavrina, an outstanding artist from the Ukraine. New and interesting work is also being done by Maj Mituric, E. Monin and

Walter Grieder, «Die Geburtstagsreise», Freiburg i. Br. 1961

Algirdas Steponavicius, an artist from Lithuania whose style combines a strong sense of folk-lore with a technique that tends towards abstraction.

The other countries of Eastern Europe are represented here by Yugoslavia, Czechoslovakia, and Poland, and they all exhibit a stylistic movement which stands in a vital relationship to contemporary developments in the liberal arts. Most nations, but above all the Poles and the Czechs, build upon powerful traditions of their own, whose roots in the past remain intact and which indeed admit a certain degree of influence from the nowadays somewhat despised field of popular art. Before and during the Second World War both Poland and Czechoslovakia produced some remarkable illustrators, among whom I need only call to mind Jiři Trnka★ (p. 99) and that artist steeped in tradition and popular culture, Josef Lada★ (p. 93).

Yugoslavia

Outdoing Switzerland in the diversity of her scenery and her local dialects, Yugoslavia has, since the war, vastly increased her production of books for children and, above all, picture-books. She has indeed created in them a style all her own, which mirrors the colourful variety of a predominantly rural country rich in fairy stories, folk-songs, costumes, and all sorts of strange and often light-hearted customs.

Yugoslavia has always had a wealth of poets—even poets writing for children or writing books which children can read. Artistically she has largely shared in the traditions of German-speaking countries (probably through the pervasive influence of Austria) and picture-books by such artists as Kreidolf, Gertrud Caspari, and Sybille von Olfers have been published with Yugoslavian texts. Since the twenties, however, the wealth of her own folk-tales has summoned a response from her own illustrators and the end of the German occupation in 1945 saw the start of a great deal of activity in the field of children's books. We are concerned here only with picture-books, but these could never have arrived at their present originality if writers, and indeed poets, of the first order had not given children an early taste for the language of poetry. The vigorous extension of the traditions of nursery verse by modern poets is something which is common to all the countries of Eastern Europe.

In turning to the illustrators one finds straight away names which are beginning to mean something in the West. First and foremost—Marlenka Stupica★ who created a kind of picture-book all her own and who continues to exercise a strong influence on others. She is represented here only by a two-colour drawing from Marcel Aymé's *Les contes du chat perché* (p. 40), but this hits off exactly the pictorial charm which keys in with the style of Yugoslavian children's literature. Ančka Gošnik-Godec★ and Marija Vogelnik★ (pp. 130 and 165) show a stronger tendency towards expressionism, while the fairy-

Paul Nussbaumer, «Der Knabe des Tell», Zürich 1965

tale illustrations of Lidija Osterc★ (p. 163) and Roza Sisčanec show a more stylized ornamentation. The illustration on p. 56 gives some idea of the pleasure which Yugoslavian picture-book artists take in plenty of colour. I should also mention the isolated attempts at a greater abstraction such as Ive Seljak-Čopič's bold illustrations for a pastoral tale by the Nobel prizewinner Ivo Andric (*Aska in Volk*, Mladinska Knjiga, 1963.)[1]

Czechoslovakia

The movement which today has made children's picture-books a centre of interest for educationists and artists has affected Eastern as well as Western Europe. Likewise the danger exists there too that something which sprang from necessity, not to say idealism or even love, is turning into a profitable line of business, a mere routine. Adolf Zábranský,★ for instance, next to Jiři Trnka one of the most popular illustrators in Czechoslovakia, brought a refreshing originality to the picture-books of the forties (p. 88), while today he is turning out picture-books with a rather monotonous facility. By contrast the work of Jiři Trnka★ is continuously changing. As an illustrator he is infinitely more inventive and it looks as though his grounding in puppet plays and his present activity in puppet films suits him very well. Moreover, he has been an illustrator from boyhood on—turning to it professionally in 1939 in his twenty-seventh year. In spite of his bold use of colour and form, Trnka seems to me to be a traditional artist in the best sense and it is therefore no surprise that his own five children love first and foremost the books of Josef Lada,★ the Czech illustrator whose work lies closest to the spirit of the people.

The poet among Czech illustrators is Ota Janeček★ who is able to achieve dream-like effects of great delicacy in his coloured chalk drawings for modern lyric verse (p. 7). But this is not the only field in which he has worked. He is a freelance artist of the first rank and it has been said of him that 'in difficult times' he knew how to 'maintain a bridge between the pictorial art of Czechoslovakia and the world revolution in art'. As an artist he has always taken a great delight in drawing comic little figures for his own two children, but only in 1955 did he begin to tackle book illustration seriously. His versatility as colourist and wit are seen especially clearly in one of his most recent works: a fat, fully illustrated edition of Joel Chandler Harris's *Uncle Remus*.

Apart from the work of these three artists the general level of Czech book illustration is extremely high. Besides the technique of montage which is having such a vogue at present, a part is also being played by witty caricaturists and by representatives of 'the new realism', a style which has not been fostered in Russia alone. Only a few among many names can be mentioned

[1] Almost all the artists mentioned here are Slovenes and their work is fostered by the Slovene publishing house: Mladinska Knjiga.

Emanuele Luzzati, «I Paladini di Francia», Milano 1962

here: Vladimír Hlavatý,★ the gifted illustrator of children's verse by the German poet Morgenstern (p. 119); Vladimír Fuka,★ an attractive satirist (p. 145) who is at present working on the delicate task of illustrating St. Exupéry's *Le petit prince*; and also the technically more sophisticated Dagmar Berková★ (p. 164) and Mirko Hanák, whose virtuosity with the paint-brush calls to mind the art of the Far East. The colour illustration by Arnŏst Karásek (p. 51) shows the extraordinary range of colour which distinguishes not only this example from those of Western Europe. Czechoslovakian artists can obviously call upon the services of some superb printers and lithographers. Among other artists who are rarely heard of outside their own country are the gifted illustrators Viera Bombova and Alois Klimo.

Poland

Janusz Grabiański★ is the Polish illustrator best known in the West, since his books were translated very early on. However, although he has shown himself able to tackle a multiplicity of subjects and although he is genuinely sympathetic to children, he, too, like Zábranský, is in danger of turning out books of a routine sameness—something which so easily becomes the successor to success.

Drawing by M. Bylina.

50

29

Arnošt Karásek, «Sedlákův Mlýnek», Praha 1961

But other names are also well known, such as Jan Lenica★ (p. 187), Adam Kilián★ (p. 105), and Józef Wilkoń★ (p. 190). There is delightful evidence of Polish folk-art in Adam Kilián's work and this blends in very well with the freedom of his approach.

I have already mentioned the two-man team from Poland, Lewitt–Him, who moved to England in 1938. The same year they had produced their famous illustrations for Juljan Tuwin's book *Lokomotywa*, and this has been very successfully re-illustrated by Jan Lenica (p. 187).

As an illustrator of poetry Olga Siemaszko★ shows great versatility (p. 100), while our colour illustration by Jerzy Srokowski★ (p. 54) exemplifies his bold approach to the world of fairy-tale. Among other things he has illustrated an edition of *Peter Pan.*

These artists can call upon a great wealth of imaginative writing for their work, but factual books also receive public encouragement and support. In spite of the state's protection of publishing, the artistic freedom of the individual is sovereign. Poetry and fairy stories are predominant among the books produced and the penetration of realistic fiction and factual books by Communist propaganda is in no way deducible from the illustrations. We can, in fact, learn much from the single-minded activity of Eastern publishers, who, with the aid of such fine writers and illustrators, have created a world of riches for their children.

Asia

If Japan and India are the chief Asian countries to be considered in this volume, it is not without good reason. Today almost all the countries of Asia possess children's books as well as mere schoolbooks, but hardly any country has developed a style and a tradition of its own. What is usually to be found is, more or less, a derivation from the mass-produced goods of Europe and America with some thinly exotic overtones. The emergence of a need to entertain children has outrun the artist's opportunity to develop his own way of expression. The old tradition of Asian countries, for instance, that of miniature painting, was seldom adopted—perhaps because it was an art of the aristocracy, perhaps because tradition itself has been largely rejected.

India

Nevertheless, in many places movements are emerging which aim to show children something of the life and the art of their own country, and as but one example I would like to mention the efforts of a man from Delhi whose love of children has led him to set up a non-profit-making organization, *The children's book trust*, with its own publishing house, its own presses, and its own studios for illustration and for children's drawings. As publisher of India's most widely circulated satirical journal—*Shankar's weekly*—and thanks to public backing, Shankar Pillai has been able to accomplish this and the first books—Indian fairy tales illustrated by Indians—are in production. The example here (p. 74) is taken from an Indian animal legend with pictures by a Bengali.

Indian books, like most of the books throughout Asia, have got to be very cheap if they are to reach a wider public than hitherto. Shankar's experiment is a symbol of India's emancipation from the English tradition which had formerly prevailed, but it manages this without being narrowly nationalistic. And its representative—the cosmopolitan, highly educated founder and director of the undertaking—has built for it a real fairy-tale house, whose façade is decorated with a giant mosaic based upon a child's drawing.

Of course other projects are also under way to bring children pleasure and instruction through the enjoyable medium of picture-books. It is very difficult in the face of India's many-sided character to get a true picture, and it is even more difficult to recognize what is really worth while when there has been inadequate technical development. Nothing is more necessary in this

Jerzy Srokowski
«Wesołe Historie»
Warszawa 1957

field than the training of printers and other people professionally concerned with books. There is certainly no lack of writers nor indeed of illustrators.

While the German-language edition of this book was in the press a new series of books appeared—*A Kamal Kitab* (Lotus books), edited by Om Prakash and published by Jajkamal Prakashan, a dedicated educational publisher in Delhi. There are a number of fine illustrators at work in this series which is meeting the demands for both entertainment and instruction. There is, for instance, the story of a little girl who would like to be a dancer—a truly Indian subject—which is told by a famous dancer and correspondingly well illustrated. Other volumes have pictures by well-known press artists, while books about the geography and history of India take special account in both pictures and text of the youngest readers in villages, for whom up to this time there has been little produced except the standard schoolbooks. The editor who is seeking to base his standards on the best European publications nevertheless seems to be striving for a typically Indian style, just as Shankar Pillai is doing with his *Children's book trust*.

This desire for independence is current throughout the whole of Asia, but everywhere there is a lack of the right sort of money in the right sort of places and a lack of printers and publishers and often of illustrators too.

China
As represented by the two popular picture-strips here (pp. 175 and 176) China may be thought to be producing illustrations which are still in the completely traditional style of the plentiful fairy-story books which are mostly charming, if cheap, imitations of the old art of the Chinese woodcut. Modern stories have been illustrated in a conventionally naturalistic manner, often with a leaning towards Russian examples. The spirit of the new China does not seem to have fostered any startling new direction in art, but the upheavals of the present cultural revolution make it very difficult to forecast anything even of the immediate future. By and large, however, the children of China have a great many cheap booklets to choose from, ranging from pure entertainment through all kinds of instructional material to pure Communist doctrine.

Hongkong
Even in the English colony of Hongkong, where you can buy both Communist and non-Communist books for children, it is possible to find lots of compact, bright little paperbacks and picture-story books, some of them excellent reading primers, but nothing indicative of a vigorous revival. Naturally picture-books from the best English publishers are available in the bookshops, but you can also find comic picture-strips here of American, English, and

Milan Bizovičar, «Prvi Maj», Ljubljana 1961

Chinese origin, for even Communist China cannot help producing such universally understandable stuff (p. 175).

Japan

Outside Europe and all the English-speaking countries, Japan is the only country which stands on its own feet in the production of illustrated children's books; a country, indeed, whose wealth of books exceeds that of many European lands. The history of children's books in Japan is still to be written, but every student of the arts knows of her famous picture-scrolls, which date from around the year A.D. 1100. These yard-long strips of paper contain stories in which words and pictures blend together with a remarkable unity. It would be odd if a country which created such things in past centuries were not in the process of devising children's picture-books of an individual stamp.

Present-day Japanese children are voracious readers. You have only to travel in a train to see this. Everyone standing will have his eyes glued to a paperback or some other little book which will be one among several bought for next to nothing from the bookstall, straightway to be immured in the depths of a closed bag. As in most parts of the world these books are largely banal productions even if they do have an exotic charm for Western eyes.

Nevertheless, the concern for good children's books dates back now for a good half century. In 1908, that is to say forty years after Japan began to convert herself into a modern state on Western lines and thirty years after compulsory schooling had been introduced, there appeared the first series of modern picture-books under the title of *Otogi-Gacho* (*Fairy-tales*). Another series, *Kodomo no Tomo* (*Children's friend*), which is also a kind of newspaper with liberal educational inclinations, has been appearing since 1914, and a further newspaper, *Kodomo no Kuni* (*Children's country*), since 1922. Both of these have had the co-operation of some excellent illustrators, who in the past have been strongly influenced by European artists such as Arthur Rackham, Edmund Dulac, and Walter Trier. From 1927 onwards a home-produced range of kindergarten picture-books has been prominent, many of which deal with factual subjects in cheap single booklets of pictures. In this way for some decades an ever-increasing weight of educational and artistic effort has been opposing the powerful force of commercial mass-production and, as time passes, its influence is being felt.

Without doubt the invasion by Western culture which has been officially fostered since 1868 has given rise to a dilemma, not only in causing Japanese children to wear European sailor-suits as school uniform—even down to the present day—but also in its permeation of their literary and visual world. On the one hand, they have accepted the heritage of Western children's literature from *Heidi*, *Alice*, *Winnie-the-Pooh* to the American comic-strips, while many of their parents know all about the educational teachings of, say, Pestalozzi or the German idea of the kindergarten. On the other hand, this is a country without illiteracy and with a special regard for its own traditional idea of the family, where the children (and especially the sons) are the little lords and masters and where the place of the women—the mothers and grandmothers— is still largely in the home. Under these circumstances there can be no lack of story-tellers and fairy-tale tellers, nor yet of illustrators too, and their work may well be based on indigenous material.

Since 1938 the state has committed itself to preventing the production of trash, but at that date there was a horrifying increase in nationalist propaganda, especially in children's books. The coming of the Second World War terminated any progressive developments that were taking place and a considerable time elapsed until, after the war, a new trend showed itself. The interest in all things foreign which had been so typical before, now penetrated into picture-books. The worlds of European fairy stories, of Negro fairy stories, of African hunters' tales, and Indian mythology were transported into Japanese picture-books in a singularly exciting way. I refer to such picture-book series as those published by Fukuinkan Shoten and Shiko-Sha, who have even set out to produce a version of the Bible for small children, illustrated in the grand manner. The publishing house Kobunsha has produced some richly illustrated retellings of ancient Japanese fairy stories, while there is a widely varied production of books on subjects dealing with natural history.

The examples in this book have all been taken from the series *Kodomo no Tomo*, where true Japanese tradition is combined with modern artistic styles without any provincial narrowness. This selection has come about largely because the series was the first which came to my notice and because it carried information about its contents written in English. It could thus be studied for the value of its content, while other series could only be judged on purely visual considerations. These seven examples make up only a small portion of a series expressly planned for children of kindergarten age. It has been carried through with initial losses but with gathering success by a group of young, unblinkered editors, fairy-tale collectors and story-tellers who have inspired their illustrators to produce children's picture-books which breach the old conventions and which may stand as an example to many countries who have yet to make a start in this field.

The artists Seiichi Horiuchi* (p. 159), Suekichi Akaba* (p. 194), and Y. Segawa have given bold new forms to old fairy stories and legends. Tadayoshi Yamamoto* (p. 188) and Michinori Murata* (p. 182) are outstanding illustrators of technical subjects which have a great following in modern Japan and which they invest with a peculiar quality of animation rather like that found in the railway picture-books by English illustrators. Chiyoko Nakatani* is a young artist whose work is already gaining a foothold in Europe—*Hippopotamus* (p. 62) has been published in France, Switzerland, England, and the United States. But she has also created a series of fine animal books which have a great appeal to children without descending to childishness or sentimentality. Haruo Yamanaka,* with a picture-story (p. 122) which bears resemblances to the old picture-scrolls, stands as a witness that even traditional representational methods can enjoy a vigorous revival.

Introduction to the Illustrations

This compilation is the result of some reflection and of many years activity as a book-collector; at the same time it represents a kind of extension to the discussion of picture-books which took place in *Three centuries of children's books in Europe*.

Apart from my own collection of children's books I was able to call upon the copious private library of contemporary picture-books assembled by Mrs. Elisabeth Waldmann in Zürich. I am greatly indebted to her enormous knowledge of the subject, for much good advice, as well as for her work on the bio-bibliographical supplement. I have also been greatly stimulated by visiting many exhibitions, above all, the various national exhibitions arranged by the International Children's Library at Munich.

My original intention in making this collection was to give some idea of the variety that there was in children's book illustration, especially in picture-books published since the Second World War. All countries where some kind of artistic renaissance had taken place in the last twenty years were to be represented. During the time that I was carrying out this design, however, so many really astonishing examples were published that I had to modify my original plan a good deal.

Instead, I am now trying primarily to give an idea of how the world, or certain parts of it, reveals itself to a present-day child through his picture-books and out of this idea has developed the following anthology of pictures, arranged by subject. After all sorts of other trial arrangements this seemed to me to be the one most suitable for giving an impression of the riches of the 'picture-book world'. Twenty-two countries are represented here, the number of examples from each depending upon the variety of its picture-book production. Some countries, indeed some continents, have been left out altogether. In spite of all efforts it has not been possible to obtain a proper notion of the kind of work that they are producing in this field. However, I hope that a future edition will represent Australia as well as the countries of South America and Africa, where many promising developments are coming to the fore. Quite a lot of countries, especially in the Near East, can point to their own production of picture-books but without having a style of their own. There is still a lot of work to be done on this score.

Without exception the countries of Europe are making tremendous efforts today to offer children the best they can, but even so not all of them are represented here— nor yet every European artist who deserves to be. The material available is so infinitely varied that I would have had no difficulty in making a case for a book interchangeable with this one but based on completely different titles and, quite possibly, on different illustrators. The book that has emerged, however, with its variety of information in pictures, text, and bibliography, would not have done so without the help of numerous friends in all parts of the globe: of artists who gave information so freely about their work, of helpful colleagues among publishers, who provided me with good advice, with catalogues and other particulars, and also of those Czech, Yugoslavian, Swedish, Danish, Italian, and German publishers who made the colour illustrations possible by supplying the appropriate transparencies.

The introductory text has been illustrated with views of 'children reading' from all parts of the world. Original drawings for this purpose by Maurice Sendak, Chyoko Nakatani, and Marianne Scheel were placed at my disposal by the artists themselves and I am deeply grateful to them. The other drawings were taken from various children's books and are acknowledged on the next pages.

The foregoing colour illustrations and the following monochrome ones have all been given full publication details based upon information in the original editions. Where translations into English or, failing that, German have been made these are given in the bio-bibliographical supplement. This supplement also shows the American publishers of English examples and vice versa.

It was not practicable to acknowledge in the text the sources of the line-drawings of children reading; these came from the following books:

p. 13 Lilo Fromm. *Das Kinderhaus*, by Ingrid Bachér. Freiburg, Atlantis, 1965.

p. 15 Romulus Candea. *Der alte und der junge und der kleine Stanislaus*, by Vera Ferra-Mikura. Vienna, Jungbrunnen, 1962.

p. 16 Felix Hoffmann. *Joggeli wott go Birli schüttle*. Aarau, Sauerländer, 1963.

p. 23 Ilon Wikland. *Madicken*, by Astrid Lindgren. Stockholm, Raben & Sjögren, 1960.

p. 26 Ernest Shepard. *Ben and Brock*. London, Methuen, 1965.

p. 30 William Papas. *No mules*. London, Oxford University Press, 1967.

p. 35 Ugo Fontana. *Storie dell'Angelo Custode*, by Laura Draghi. Florence, Vallecchi, 1959.

p. 37 Lorenzo Goñi. *Rocinante de la Mancha*, by Miguel Buñuel. Madrid, Editora Nacional, 1963.

p. 41 Annick Delhumeau. *Contes d'agate*, by Micheline Maurel. Paris, Hatier, 1960.

p. 50 Michał Bylina. *Czarodziejska Księga*, by Janina Porazińska. Warsaw, Nasza Księgarnia, 1961.

The original drawings by Marianne Scheel mentioned on the last page appear on pp. 5 and 9, those by Chiyoko Nakatani on pp. 52 and 58, and that by Maurice Sendak on p. 18.

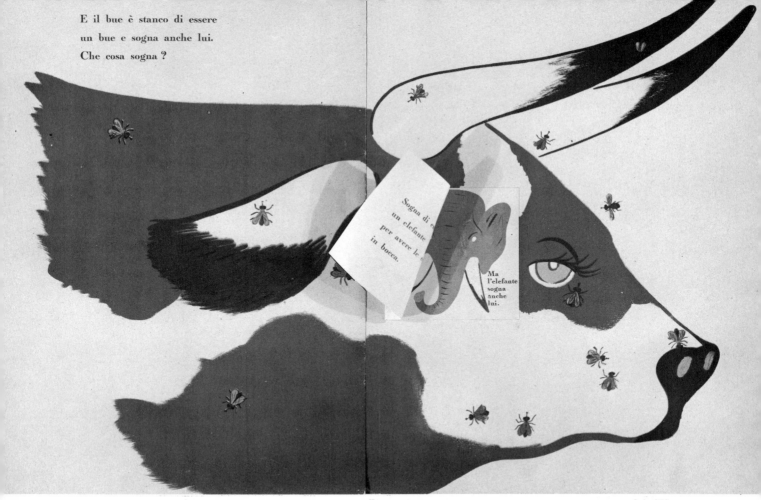

E il bue è stanco di essere
un bue e sogna anche lui.
Che cosa sogna ?

Sogna di e
un elefante
per avere le
in bocca.

Ma
l'elefante
sogna
anche
lui.

Bruno Munari. *Mai contenti*. Milan, Mondadori, 1945.

Animals in Picture-Books

From the early editions of Aesop to Brian Wildsmith's *Wild Animals*, animals have been the most popular inhabitants of picture-books and their presentation has similarly ranged from mythical fantasy to biological exactness. The ox shown here has thoughts of becoming an elephant, as can be seen by lifting the flap and looking inside his head. This is an early post-war example of the many attempts that have been made to turn the conventional picture-book into a plaything as well.

かばより　ちいさい　かばのこ
かばのこより　ちいさい　かめのこ
かめより　ちいさいもの　なんだ？
あぶく………

Chiyoko Nakatani. *Hippopotamus* by Eriko Kishida. Tokyo, Fukuinkan-Shoten, 1962.

Sureness of taste and sensitivity towards the natural world are characteristics of East Asian picture-books. They are exemplified here in the restrained but life-like drawing and the feeling for page design. Mathiesen's boldly stylized 'blue-eyed cat' (right) stands in strong contrast, but has been exceedingly popular.

Egon Mathiesen. *Mis med de blå Øjne*.
Copenhagen, Gyldendal, 1949.

Marc Simont. *The happy day* by Ruth Krauss. New York, Harper, 1949.

Every morning they hopped out of bed
and out into the early morning sunshine.

Garth Williams. *The rabbits' wedding.* New York, Harper, 1958.

Two very similar approaches to the natural world from America. In both cases the fantasy of the story is given an added dimension by the accuracy of the illustrations.

Mool spaziert durch die Gänge. Alles ist still und dunkel.

Mal schnuppert er hier, mal lauscht er da.

Klaus Winter and Helmut Bischoff. *Mool.* Freiburg, Herder, 1962.

Celestino Piatti. *Eulenglück* by T. van Hoijtema. Zürich, Artemis, 1965.

Reality has here been adapted to meet the needs of a graphic method. In its
turn the method helps to bring out significant detail (left) or to make a picture
out of the familiar techniques of close-up photography.

Wilhelm Jaruska. *Alle meine Pferde* by Alexis Steiner. Vienna, Jugend und Volk, 1963

Two comments on horses. Jaruska has chosen an expressionist style to portray a scene of animal savagery; Helen Kasser's romantic approach is more appropriate to Kipling's fable.

Helen Kasser. *Die Katze, die für sich allein ging* (*The cat who walked by himself*) by Rudyard Ki... Zürich, Artemis, 1961.

Rainey Bennett. *After the sun goes down.* Cleveland, World, 1961.

In the past owls and lions have been regarded as sinister as well as dangerous beasts; in recent years they have both been reformed into fashionable and sympathetic picture-book heroes.

Roger Duv
The happy lion by Louise
New York, Whittlesey,

Josephine had never seen such a ragged, untidy animal and was sure if her friends saw him they would laugh.

Gerald Rose. *Wuffles goes to town* by Elizabeth Rose. London, Faber, 1959.

Oleg Zinger. *Ist das ein Löwe?* by Ilse Windmüller. Berlin, Kinderbuchverlag, 1950.

Two comments on dogs. An English caricature of an English pet and an East German illustration for a book which considers different breeds and their usefulness to men.

की बात मानूंगा। जिस सिलसिले से तुम लोगों ने अपने को भेंट किया है उसी सिलसिले से खाना शुरू करूंगा।"

यह सुनकर गिद्द, लोमड़ी और चीता सन्न रह गए। भला वह ऐसा कब चाहते थे?

गिद्द उड़ गया। लोमड़ी और चीता भाग गए। वह फिर कभी उस जंगल में नहीं दीखे।

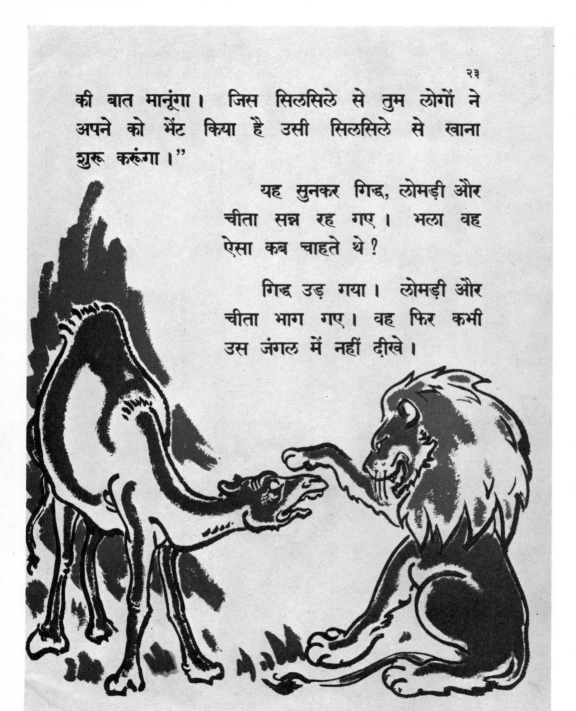

The king's choice. The Children's Book Trust, Delhi, 1963.

One of the first attempts to provide Indian children with a home-produced picture-book. The illustration is by a Bengal artist.

Dann lernte ich, wie man Wasser
trinkt. Ich tauchte meinen Rüssel
in den Teich, saugte das Wasser auf
und spritzte es mir in den Mund.

Als nächstes lernte ich, wie
man ein Brausebad nimmt.
Ob man sich nun von außen
wäscht oder von innen, es ist

fast das gleiche. So kam es mir
wenigstens vor, denn mei-
nen Rüssel gebrauchte ich
ja immer, ob ich Wasser

Ruprecht Haller. *Mora* by Mulk Raj Anand. Berlin, Holz, 1960.

Illustrations by a German artist for a tale by another Indian writer.

M. Jimenez Arnalot. *Yo soy el gato* by L. R. Fabra. Barcelona, Gama, 1963.

Stylization can be applied with varying degrees of success. The cat on the left is extraordinarily true to life, while the complex perspective in the Italian drawing may detract from the child's enjoyment of the picture's vigour and colour.

Giancarlo Carloni and Giulio Cingoli. *Il fagiano Gaetano* by G. Rocca. Milan, Mursia, 1961.

But Peter, sitting in the tree, said: 'Don't shoot! The bird and I have caught the wolf. Now help us to take him to the zoo.' And there imagine the triumphant procession:

27

Alan Howard. *Peter and the wolf* by Sergei Prokofiev. London, Faber, 1951.

An English and a Russian artist here demonstrate widely differing approaches to two Russian animal fables.

Yuri A. Vasnetsov. *Magpie, Magpie!* Foreign Languages Publishing House, Moscow, 1959.

The little white hen picked up her basket, and the soldier picked up the little white hen. Tramp, tramp, tramp. He threw her in the goose-run.

William Stobbs. *The little white hen* by Anita Hewett. London, Bodley Head, 1962.

Examples from England and West Germany of attempts to adapt something of the child's own way of painting to picture-books. Perspective is abandoned in favour of building up scenes in carefully arranged patches of flat, bright colour.

Katharina Maillard.
Der Kleine Herr Pucha
by Hanna Hanisch.
Oldenburg, Stalling, 1963.

Lili Roth-Streiff. *Das Rösslein Kilian* by M. Paur-Ulrich. Zürich, Atlantis, 1944.

These examples from popular picture-books from three European countries demonstrate how different approaches, from the conventional to the highly stylized, may all achieve success.

Oili Tanninen. *Miiru menee kalaan*. Helsinki, Kustannusosakeyhtiö Otava, 1961.

Wiltrud Roser. *Die Pimpelmaus*. Freiburg, Atlantis, 1958.

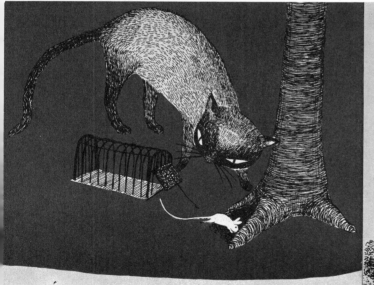

Papamaus und Mamamaus freuen sich sehr,
daß sie Pimpelmaus wieder haben.

Du darfst nie wieder in das Haus gehen,
das ist viel zu gefährlich.
Sagt Mamamaus.

Du mußt der Katze immer aus dem Weg gehen,
denn das nächste Mal frißt sie dich ganz bestimmt.
Sagt Papamaus.

Als es hell wird, kommt die Katze
und will Pimpelmaus fressen.
Sie schleicht sich an die Falle
und macht mit der Pfote die Türe auf.
Schwupp – springt Pimpelmaus heraus
und ins Mausloch hinein.

she tucked him in and said goodnight.
And she always remembered — she never forgot—
to leave him water to drink
and some hay and some oats because

Three examples of the work of Maurice Sendak which demonstrate the versatility which has made him one of the most exciting illustrators at work today.

Maurice Sendak. *Charlotte and the white horse* by Ruth Krauss. New York, Harper, 1955.

Maurice Sendak. *Little bear* by Else Holmelund Minarik. New York, Harper, 1957.

till Max said "BE STILL!"
and tamed them with the magic trick

Maurice Sendak. *Where the wild things are.* New York, Harper, 1963.

The key to Sendak's attractiveness lies in the way he combines pen-drawing and colour-wash and the command which this gives him over detail and atmosphere. He is able to adapt his technique to the demands of a given text, whether of his own devising or not.

Colette Portal. *Das Leben einer Königin*. Munich, Bilderbuchverlag, 1962.

Heinrich aber verabschiedete sich

vom Eisbären,

vom Löwen,

vom Elefanten

und vom Kamel.

Dann trabte er in die Winternacht.

Sachte fiel der Schnee.

Subjects apart, the contrast between these two pictures stems from the natural differences of the water-colour artist working in pictorial terms and the graphic artist developing a style from the traditions of the woodcut.

Werner Klemke. *Hirsch Heinrich* by Fred Rodrian. Berlin, Kinderbuchverlag, 1960.

Brum, brum, brum,
to je shon a šum!
Kdo má nerad hudbu muší,
ať si zacpe obě uši,
ať si zavře dům.

Adolf Zábranský. *Sládek dětem* by Josef V. Sládek. Prague, S.N.D.K., 1946.

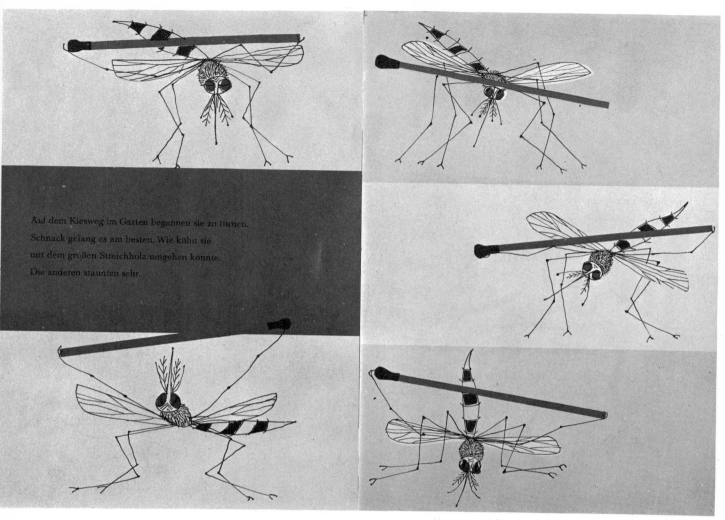

Auf dem Kiesweg im Garten begannen sie zu turnen.
Schnack gelang es am besten. Wie kühn sie
mit dem großen Streichholz umgehen konnte.
Die anderen staunten sehr.

Gerhard Oberländer. *Die Schnake Schnack*. Munich, Betz, 1963.

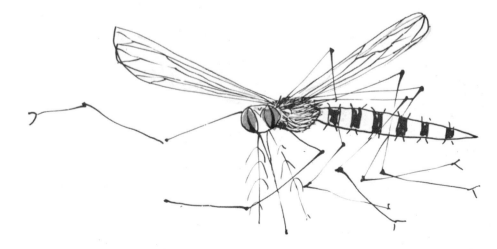

Two insect comedies. For all the differences of style and intention each artist has based his anthropomorphic version upon careful observation.

„Das ist die eine Erdhälfte", sagte der Elefant zu seiner Frau. „Und überall herr-
schen unter den Menschen Not und Unvernunft. Das sieht jedes Tier . . ."

„Nur ein Tier", sagte der Elefant, „will das Elend und Durcheinander nicht sehen —
das ist der Vogel Strauß. Er steckt den Kopf in den Sand."

Walter Trier. *Die Konferenz der Tiere* by E. Kästner and J. Lepman. Zürich, Europa, 1949.

Animals are here shown
in situations which com-
ment upon the world of
man seen in political and
technological terms.

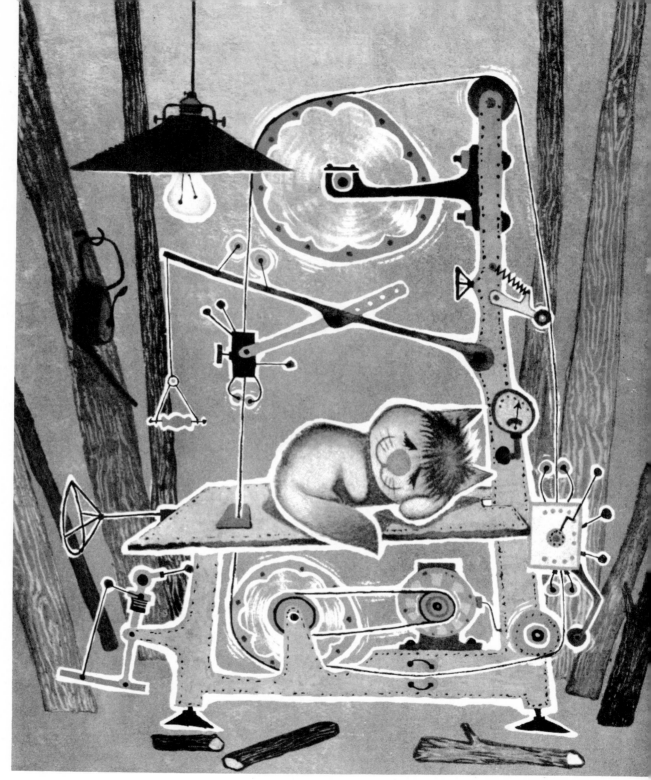

Ennio di Majo. *L' inviata specialissima* by Gina Anguissola. Milan, Mursia, 1959.

F. Haacken. *Peter und der Wolf* by S. Prokofiev. Berlin, Holz, 1958.

Two further treatments of animals in fable. This dramatic version of *Peter and the wolf* contrasts strongly with that of Alan Howard on p. 78.

Janosch. *Reineke Fuchs*. Munich, Lentz, 1962.

Rhymes and Pictures

Řípa se vdávala,
celer výskal,
mrkev tancovala
a křen pískal.

Josef Lada. *Říkadla.*
Prague, S.N.D.K., 1961.

Marijke Doornekamp. *Oude Rijmpjes*. The Hague, Van Goor, 1963.

Slaap, kindje, slaap

Slaap, kindje, slaap.
Daar buiten loopt een schaap.
Een schaap met vier witte voetjes,
Dat drinkt z'n melk zo zoetjes.
Witte wol, zwarte wol,
Kindje, drinkt z'n buikje vol.

Groen, groen grasje

Groen, groen grasje,
Melk in mijn tasje,
Melk in mijn kommetje,
Dag, mijn zoete jongetje.

53

Så rart!

Så rart å være flaggermus
og flakse rundt fra hus til hus
og gå til sengs i trærne.
Men er det noen som forstår
hvordan den kan få sove når
den henger etter tærne?

Så rart å være edderkopp
med nøste i sin egen kropp
og spinne alle dage.
Men hvordan kan den gjemme på
så mange kilometer tråd
i slik en liten mage?

Paul Gauguin. *Så rart* by Inger Hagerup. Oslo, Aschehoug, 1959.

Every page opening should display both verse and illustrations to the best advantage, as in these two examples from Holland and Norway.

Tonje Strøm Aas.
Bilder, rim og regler.
Oslo, Aschehoug, 1962.

Der kommer mennene

Vond tid, matløs tid
plager oss alle.
Sulten mage,
tomme fat ...

Ser du langt der borte?
Der kommer mennene.
Herlige seler
sleper de med seg.
Nå blir det plutselig
mat-tid igjen.
Fest og glede,
og alle er venner.
Kjenner du hvor godt det lukter
fra boblende gryter?
Og smellfett spekk
kan vi stappe i oss.
Med latter og rop
hilser vi dem
som fylte grytene våre.

(Eskimodikt)

24

Morgens früh um zehne
Holt sie Holz und Späne,
Feuert an um elfe,
Kocht sie bis um zwölfe
Fröschebein und Krebs und Fisch.
Hurtig, Kinder, kommt zu Tisch!

Typical pages from the nursery-rhyme books of three northern countries where nursery rhymes seem to flourish to a greater extent than in the south.

Helga Henschen. *Festen i Hulabo*
by Britt G. Halqvist. Lund, Gleerups, 1961.

Men kon hon pratade en stund
med slaktarns gamla trötta hund.

Han sa: — Jag dansar inte jass,
för att jag har en dålig tass.

Och så har jag förkylt min svans
och tycker det är dumt med dans.

Men ska vi skälla, du och jag,
på månen, säj, ett litet slag?

— Jag skäller ej, jag säger mu,
sa kon, och jag vill dansa nu!

Marianne Scheel. *Das Bucklig Männlein.*
Freiburg, Atlantis, 1964.

The first to come in was a little white moth,
To spread on the tablecloth.

Feodor Rojankovsky. *Frog went a-courtin'* by J. Langstaff. New York, Harcourt, Brace, 1955.

Hra v kuličky

Zdálo se mi, zdálo:
mám kuliček málo.
Chtěl jsem jich mít víc
a teď nemám nic.

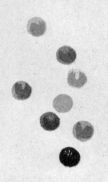

Jiři Trnka. *Říkejte si se mnou* by František Hrubín. Prague, Melantrich, 1946.

LEFT: An American folk-song illustrated by an artist born in Imperial Russia.

ABOVE: A masterpiece of Czech book production. Despite the diverse developments in his style Trnka has rarely surpassed this achievement of 1946.

LECI... LECI...

Leci, leci pszczoła
do Wojtaszka czoła...
Wojtek śpi.

Leci, leci osa
do Wojtaszka nosa...
Wojtek śpi.

Leci, leci mucha
do Wojtaszka ucha...
Wojtek śpi.

Leci bąk tłuściutki
do Wojtaszka bródki...
— A tuś mi!

Olga Siemaszko. *Wotjusiowey Izbie* by Janina Porazinska. Warsaw, Czytelnik, 1958.

Κόκκινη κλωστὴ στριμένη
στὴν ἀνέμη γυρισμένη...
παραμύθι μᾶς ἀρχίζει
κι ὅλους μὲ χαρὰ γεμίζει.

Τὸ τσουκάλι σιγοβράζει.
Τὰ κλαδιὰ ἔξω ταράζει
ὁ ἀγέρας δυνατά,
καὶ ὁ σκύλος ἀλυχτᾶ.

Louisa Montesantou. (*Our little house*) by Pipinas Zimikali. Athens, Astir, 1951.

LEFT: A typical page from a Polish picture-book by one of the best-known Polish artists.

ABOVE: One of the best examples from a country with few outstanding picture-books.

The Wart Hog

The wart hog's face is a disgrace,
His shape is like a jar,
He's never welcome any place,
Where well-dressed people are.

But look at him with kindly eyes,
And you will find, I'm told,
That though he'll win no beauty prize,
His heart is purest gold.

7

Alice and Martin Provensen. *The animal book.* New York, Golden Press, 1952.

A wise old owl lived in an oak;
The more he saw the less he spoke.
The less he spoke the more he heard:
Why can't we all be like that wise old bird?

47

Brian Wildsmith. *Mother Goose*. London, Oxford University Press, 1964.

Famous illustrators and their sharply contrasting treatment of popular rhymes.

Der Sommer

Er trägt einen Bienenkorb als Hut,
blau weht sein Mantel aus Himmelsseide,
die roten Füchse im gelben Getreide
kennen ihn gut.
Sein Bart ist voll Grillen. Die seltsamsten Mären
summt er der Sonne vor, weil sie's mag,
und sie kocht ihm dafür jeden Tag
Honig und Beeren.

Johannes Grüger. *Die Sternenmühle* by Christine Busta. Salzburg, Müller, 1959.

Summer and Sun

Adam Kilian. *Zajęczy Pałac* by Anna Kamieńska. Warsaw, Czytelnik, 1962.

Drawing faces on the heavenly bodies is a temptation to artists as well as schoolboys. The above example is from a Polish version of the fable of the North Wind and the Sun.

Northern tradition depicts the sun as rubicund and benign. A Mediterranean version (right) suggests some of his more hostile attitudes.

Eva Johanna Rubin. *3 × 3 an einem Tag* by James Krüss. Munich, Betz, 1963.

P. Shaar. (*Three little cats*) by Bella Baram. Tel-Aviv, Massadah, n.d.

A Sequence of Ships

John Burningham. *Borka*. London, Cape, 1963.

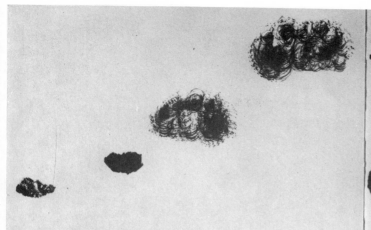

2

Und ich tanzte auf einer Brücke und sah hinunter in das dunkle Wasser. Ein Schiff kam gefahren. Ganz tief lag es im Wasser, denn es war voll beladen. Mein Bruder Heinrich stand ganz vorn und schwang eine große Glocke. Und jedes Bimm und jedes Bamm wurde zu einer Wolke und flog leise in den blauen Himmel. Ich wollte rufen und mitfahren, aber das Schiff machte nicht halt auf der unbekannten Reise.

Liselotte Schwarz. *Leiermann dreht goldne Sterne*. Hamburg, Ellermann, 1959.

The solidity of Burningham's coaster is in the best Masefield tradition and its bulk contrasts strongly with the fantasy of the dream-ship (above) which has been composed through the medium of cut-paper work.

Kathleen Hale. *Orlando, the marmalade cat.* London, Country Life, 1952.

Orlando's holiday houseboat can still be seen at Aldeburgh and has a degree of authenticity quite lacking in the vessel in Poul Strøyer's nonsense story.

Poul Strøyer. *Bytt är bytt.* Stockholm, Almqvist, 1960.

But you can imagine his dismay, for when he arrived at the quayside he saw the *Amelia Jane* steaming out to sea. He had missed his ship.

Edward Ardizzone. *Tim all alone*. London, Oxford University Press, 1956.

Ardizzone at his most typical—observation and knowledge wedded to an impeccable water-colourist's style.

Die Sonne zog ein grau Gesicht,
denn so ein Protz, der paßt ihr nicht,

und plötzlich fing's zu regnen an,
um unsern Schimmel war's getan.

Beatrice Braun-Fock. *Der schwarze Schimmel* by Ernst Heimeran. Munich, Betz, 1956.

Rain and Snow

Karla Kuskin. *James and the rain*. New York, Harper, 1957.

Rain developed into a pictorial joke. . . .

Sigrid Heuck. *Pony* by Gina Ruck-Pauquèt. Freiburg, Atlantis, 1961.

. . . . and snow used to accentuate a sense of security.

The expressionism of an artist who is a master of woodcut techniques brings out the violence of bad weather—not always recognized in children's books.

Antonio Frasconi. *The snow and the sun—la nieve y el sol*. New York, Harcourt, Brace, 1961.

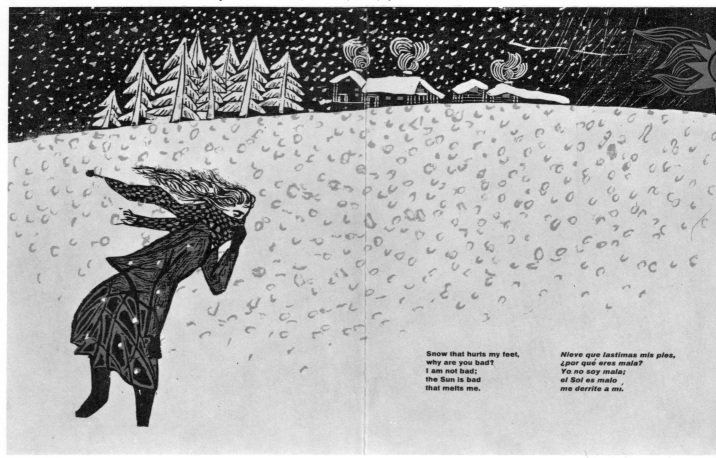

Snow that hurts my feet,
why are you bad?
I am not bad;
the Sun is bad
that melts me.

Nieve que lastimas mis pies,
¿por qué eres mala?
Yo no soy mala;
el Sol es malo
me derrite a mi.

The snow came down
And covered the ground,
And the two little trains going West.

And they got white and furry,
And still in a hurry
They puffed and chugged to the West.

Jean Charlot. *Two little trains* by Margaret Wise Brown. New York, W. R. Scott, 1949.

Tomi Ungerer. *Snail, where are you?* New York, Harper, 1962.

Snow and water used for an almost entirely decorative purpose.

Soon clouds made a strange slow
swirling sombre sky, rain turned
everything to soft shimmering shapes,
while Bronto loved to stroll from
place to place and sense the
splishy sploshy splashy water on his face.

David McKee. *Bronto's wings*. London, Dobson, 1964.

Two further examples of rain and snow used for their pictorial qualities.

Vladimír Hlavatý. *Allerlei Tierlein* by Christian Morgenstern. Prague, S.N.D.K., 1959.

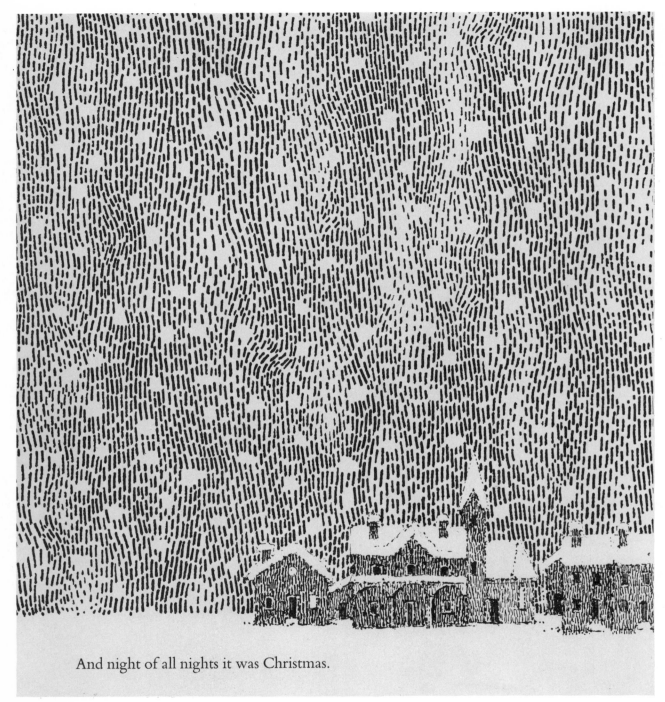

And night of all nights it was Christmas.

Beni Montresor. *On Christmas Eve* by Margaret Wise Brown. New York, Scott, 1961.

A blending of formal and atmospheric qualities to produce a completely
successful Christmas scene within the limits of the single page.

The World's Children in Picture-Books

Janusz Grabiański. *Franek* by Maria Konopnicka. Warsaw, Nasza Księgarnia, 1957.

Haruo Yamanaka. *The tops of long-nosed goblins*. Tokyo, Fukuinkan-Shoten, 1958.

Giancarlo Carloni. *Gip nel televisore* by Gianni Rodari. Milan, Mursia, 1962

There is a double satisfaction to be gained from studying the treatment of children by picture-book artists in a variety of countries. The child himself may take pleasure in recognizing correspondences to his own situation, no matter what the place or time may be. In addition, many picture-books will tell us a lot about the changing attitudes of adults towards children and the different ways in which they see them.

The two pictures here contrast very aptly the children in a traditional fairy-tale from Japan and those in a satiric modern story from Italy.

Alois Carigiet. *Uorsin* by Selina Chönz. Chur, Lia Rumantscha, 1945. *Schellen-Ursli*, Zürich, Schweizer Spiegel Verlag, 1945.

The warmth of a child's relationship to adults within the family is here contrasted with the unnerving gap that may suddenly open when questions of authority or experience are raised.

Barbara Dutkowska. *Kozucha Kłamczucha* by Janina Porazińska. Warsaw, Nasza Księgarnia, 1956.

Françoise. *The big rain*. New York, Scribners, 1961.

Vladimir V. Lebedev. *The three bears* by Lev Tolstoi. Moscow, Foreign Publishing House, 1950.

Despite the wide divergence of nationality and graphic technique there is a striking similarity in the portraiture of these two country girls.

From an Indian alphabet. Bombay, K. B. Dhawale for Mayur Kitaben, 1954.

Mother and child prepare the family meal—in the pages of an Indian alphabet and in one of the Père Castor series of picture-books about children of other lands.

Paul–Emile Victor. *Apoutsiak, le petit flocon de neige.* Paris, Flammarion, 1948.

A cinq ans, Petit-flocon-de-neige mangeait comme un ogre.

De toutes ses petites dents il mordait dans la viande que sa mère lui donnait.

Voici un coin de la grande hutte de pierre où toute la famille d'Apoutsiak vit en hiver. La maman d'Apoutsiak vient de faire cuire de la viande de phoque sur la lampe à huile.

Apoutsiak et sa maman sont accroupis sur une plateforme de bois qui leur sert tantôt de table, tantôt de lit. Au-dessus d'eux, une peau de phoque sèche, tendue sur un cadre.

Ančka Gošnik-Godec. *Levi Devžej* by Prežihov Voranc. Ljubljana, Mladinska Knjiga, 1962.

Farmer's children drawn from the childhood memories of a Yugoslav poet and from the contemporary realism of a Spanish writer.

Celedonio Perellón. *Colasin y Colason* by J. M. Sanchez-Silva. Madrid, Editora Nacional, 1963.

In both pictures simplification almost to the point of caricature serves to increase the directness of the visual impact.

Micheline Chevallier. *Yo, le petit Tibétain*. Paris, Hatier, 1962.

Despite the difference in graphic treatment, both of these pictures are true to the spirit of the Tibetan and Siamese surroundings which they portray.

Jacqueline Ayer. *A wish for little sister*. New York, Harcourt, Brace, 1960.

This is where Little Sister lives
in a brown wooden house.
Its dark, cool rooms are filled
with the colors of silk.

Every morning when Little Sister wakes up,
she hears the sounds of the big looms on which the silk is woven.
  "Picket pocket slide shut
  Picket pocket slide shut,"
the big looms clatter away.

Sur le chemin de l'école, Marie rencontra un petit âne gris qui cherchait un chardon pour son déjeuner et n'en trouvait pas.

Marie vit ce petit âne, le petit âne la vit et tourna vers elle sa tête timide. On ne sait pas comme cela se fit, mais un magnifique chardon bleu vint tout à coup piquer le menton du petit âne.

Une grande fille vint la trouver à la récréation, et dit: "Marie, je suis malheureuse". Ma-

Pascale Claude-Lafontaine. *La fille au sourire* by H. de Saint-Blanquat. Paris, Hatier, 1962.

A cosy pastoral scene in the French tradition.

A. Gitz-Johansen. *Gaba, den lille Grønlaender.* Copenhagen, Gyldendal, 1947.

Child and wilderness—the appeal of the exotic in one of Denmark's most famous picture-books.

A strong young warrior swam across to carry Little-Feather back to safety.

Great-Eagle waited on the bank, his tomahawk in his hand.

"Now can I have the big feather?" Little-Feather asked. "I swam the widest river. That proves I deserve the biggest feather in the land."

"That proves you deserve a spanking and no supper," the Chief said harshly, and sent him home to bed.

Helen Borten. *Little Big-feather* by Joseph Longstreth. New York, Abelard-Schuman, 1956.

Three different treatments of the Red Indian theme—one by an artist who is himself an Indian.

"Now you can have Little Brother."
Mother laughed and said,
"But I HAVE Little Brother.
He came into the longhouse
with you.
He is sitting by the fire."

Arnold Lobel. *Little Runner of the Longhouse* by Betty Baker. New York, Harper, 1962.

Tom Two Arrows. *Little boy Navajo* by Virginia K. Smiley. New York, Abelard-Schuman, 1954.

Ludwig Bemelmans. *Madeline and the Gypsies*. New York, The Viking Press, 1959.

However unfamiliar the surroundings the game of dressing-up has a constant appeal. The two versions of it here demonstrate the characteristic mannerisms of two artists who have been highly successful in portraying children.

Christmas had gone by, the snow had melted, the days were getting longer and Carnival time was near, when the children would put on their fancy dresses and make merry in the streets.

Already they were preparing their costumes, borrowing hats and clothes from their parents, pinning, sewing, trying on.

In the nursery school Mother Antonia helped the little ones. But the bigger children came there too to show off their costumes and to enjoy the nice warm stove.

Bettina. *Francesco and Francesca*. London, Oxford University Press, 1962.

„Und haben lauter schwarze Streifen", sagte Ture.

II

Ulf Löfgren. *Barnen i Djungeln* by A. Lindgren und Leif Krantz. Stockholm, Rabén & Sjögren, 1959.

Picture-books from Sweden and Austria show children exploring the relationship . . .

Bumpam hebt die Vorderpfoten:
„Liebes Pferd, was glaubst du bloß?
Wir sind völlig scherenlos!
Ich bin selbst zu Hause hier
ein papier-gerißnes Tier.
Wer der Bub ist, willst du wissen?
Hannes! Der hat mich gerissen.
Laß uns doch, ich bitte dich,
laß uns beide, ihn und mich,
ins gerißne Land hinein!"
Darauf öffnet sich das Tor, und das weiße Pförtnerpferdchen
wiehert freundlich: „Tretet ein!"

Susi Weigel. *Hannes und sein Bumpam* by Mira Lobe. Vienna, Jugend und Volk, 1961.

. . . between image and reality in pictures which they make themselves.

A tree is nice because it has a trunk and limbs.
We can climb the tree and see over all the yards.
We can sit on a limb and think about things.
Or play pirate ship up in the tree.

Marc Simont. *A tree is nice* by Janice May Udry. New York, Harper, 1956.

Picture-books can depict paradise for children in a single tree, or inferno
in the streets of a front-line town.

Dalibor Parać. *Kurir Dragan i Njegovo Konjče* by Anđelka Martić. Zagreb, Nasa Djeca, 1961.

Arne Ungermann.
Palle alene i Verden
by Jens Sigsgaard.
Copenhagen, 1942.

Vladimir Fuka. *Mít' a sám na světě* by Jens Sigsgaard. Prague, S.N.D.K., 1963.

An original illustration from *Paul alone in the world* and a version from the Czech edition. Each book suggests some of the disadvantages of the boy's situation (beautifully symbolized in these two pictures), but the Czech volume replaces the humour of the original with a pervasive melancholy.

Michal Efrat. (*Journey to the fields*) by Pania Bergstein. Tel-Aviv, Hakibutz Hameuchad, 1952.

Picture-books themselves depicting the world of imagination opening to children in the pages of books.

André François. *Roland* by Nelly Stéphane. Feldafing, Buchheim, 1957.

146

Barbara Cooney.
A white heron by S. O. Jewett.
New York, Crowell, 1963.

Goodnight, Earth, I'll say,
Then I'll lie down in my spaceman's bed.
The night will be
As still as stone.

Leonard Weisgard. *When I go to the moon* by Claudia Lewis. New York, Macmillan, 1961.

A nineteenth-century American child looks at the moon from the woods of Maine, while a fellow countryman (at a later date) regards the earth with a similar Romantic fervour.

The Bible as a Picture-Book

Helen Sewell. *In the beginning* by Alf Evers. New York, Macmillan, 1954.

Then God made you and me.
He made us to love
all His beautiful world.
He made us to love

the cool places and the warm places,
the light places and the dark places,
the rocks and seas,
the valleys and mountains,
the sky and the air,

Georgy Stefula. *Das Paradies*. Hamburg, Ellermann, 1955.

Two versions of the Creation, each stemming from modern ideas about art. On the left, techniques of drawing and paper-cutting are combined to build up a stylized scene almost as a child would make it; while, above, the clarity of the naïve style does not preclude a quite sophisticated approach to composition and detail.

151

Dieu dit à Noé :
« J'ai décidé de faire disparaître de la terre les hommes devenus méchants. J'ai préparé mon grand arc de la colère. Il va tomber tant d'eau sur terre que tout va être noyé; mais toi qui m'écoutes, je veux te sauver. »

Alain le Foll. *Noé* by A. M. Cocagnac. Paris, Éditions du Cerf, 1964.

Elisabeth Landen. *Noaks Ark* by Britt G. Hallqvist. Stockholm, Diakonistyrelsens, 1963.

Och djuren fick komma till arken,
hanne och hona, par om par
— hästar, hjortar och rävar,
struts, basilisk, dromedar.

What with animals and boat-building and dramatic weather scenes, *Noah and the Ark* has all the ingredients for a completely satisfying picture-book. Almost every country has its own picture retellings and these examples from France, Sweden, and America show events at three different points in the story.

Karla Kuskin. *The animals and the ark.* New York, Harper, 1958.

A ces paroles, Jonas se met à trembler de peur.

Il prend son bâton et s'enfuit en se disant : "Dieu trouvera bien quelqu'un d'autre pour faire une commission aussi dangereuse". Il arrive bientôt à un port nommé Joppé.

Jacques le Scanff. *Jonas* by A. M. Cocagnac. Paris, Cerf, 1963.

Two attempts to recapture the spirit of Old Testament times from a series of cheap but very successful French picture-books by young modern artists.

Jean Jacouton. *Le jeune David* by A. M. Cocagnac. Paris, Cerf, 1963.

Pendant quelque temps David ira habiter près du vieux roi Saül. Aujourd'hui il joue de la harpe et chante des prières en musique, qu'on nomme psaumes, pour chasser la mauvaise tristesse du cœur du vieux roi.

Reinhard Herrmann. *Die Weihnachtsgeschichte*. Gütersloh, Mohn. 1962.

The Christmas story has been retold in pictures time and again. It has received interpretations varying from the conventional (and often grossly sentimental) to the boldly modern, exemplified in, say, Roger Duvoisin's various versions, or Kurt Wendtland's setting of the story in a desert landscape, or Paul Nussbaumer's in the winter snows of Switzerland.

This example by Reinhard Herrmann is concerned with translating the marvellous simplicity of the story into pictures, and achieves its aim through a clarity of design and a sensitive use of colour, whose surface resembles a stained-glass window.

Fairy-Tales as Picture-Books

Felix Hoffmann. *Die sieben Raben*, after Grimm. Aarau, Sauerländer, 1962.

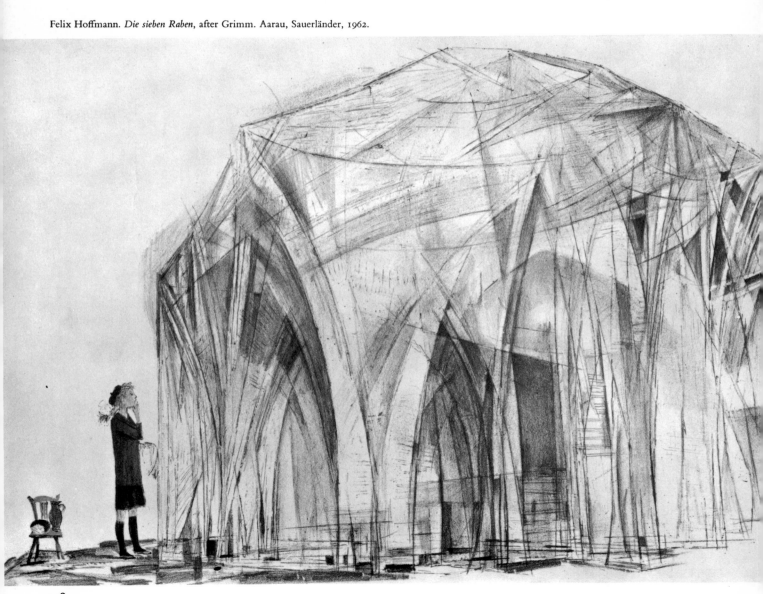

ちいさな　いもうとは、どこまでも
あるいて、とうとう、ガラスの　しろへ
つきました。しろの　もんは、ぴったり
しまって いました。むすめは、ひよこの
あしを　とりだそうとしましたが、
まあ、どうしましょう／
ながい　たびの　あいだで
なくしてしまったのです。
むすめは、ナイフで　じぶんの
こゆびを　きりました。こゆびは、
もんの　かぎに　うまく　あって、
もんの　とが　ひらきました。
すると、なかには、こびとが　ひとり
いて、「むすめさん、なにを　さがしに？」
と、たずねました。いもうとは、いいました。
「わたしの　にいさんたち。
七わの　からすを。」

Seiichi Horiuchi (*The seven ravens*), after Grimm. Tokyo, Fukuinkan-Shoten, 1959.

These two illustrations show a Swiss and a Japanese interpretation of the same incident in Grimm's story of *The seven ravens*.

The double-page spread overleaf shows Hans Fischer glossing Perrault with some ideas of his own. Cats, he argued, would not find it easy to learn to walk in boots, so this one is practising arduously in the middle of the night.

Was nicht in der Geschichte steht: nämlich, dass es für einen Kater gar nicht einfach ist, in Stiefeln zu stehen, und auf zwei Beinen zu gehen. Das musste er zuerst lernen. Und er übte heimlich in der Nacht: zuerst das Stehen, und dann das Gehen — bis es ging!

Hans Fischer. *Der gestiefelte Kater* by Charles Perrault. Zürich, Artemis, 1957.

こんどは、おおきな きに
ふくべが さがっていて、
ゆけっちゃ からから
ゆけっちゃ からから
と、なっていました。
なおも、ずんずん ゆくと、

ちいさな かわが あって、あかい かけた
おわんが、つんぷく かんぷくと、ながれて
きました。
それを ひろって、なお、ゆくと、

三ぼんの わかれみちの ところへ でました。そこには、
ささが 三ぼん はえていて、
ゆくなっちゃ がさがさ
ゆけっちゃ かさかさ と、なっていました。
そこで、一ばんまんなかの
「ゆけっちゃ かさかさ」
と、ささの なって
いる みちを
ゆくと、
とりが
すを
かけている
ところが
あり、
ゆけっちゃ とんとん
ゆけっちゃ とんとん
と、ないていました。
また、もうすこし
いくと、

Churyo Sato. (*The harvest of wild pears.*) Tokyo, Fukuinkan-Shoten, 1959.

Two magic forests; a double-page version from Japan which harks back to
the picture-scrolls, and a stylized modern forest from Yugoslavia.

Lidija Osterc. *Hišica iz Kock* by Ela Peroci. Ljubljana, Mladinska Knjiga, 1964.

Dagmar Berková. *Alenka v Kraji divů a za zrcadlem* by Lewis Carroll. Prague, S.N.D.K. 1961.

Andersen and Carroll are masters of the invented fairy-tale. The two incidents illustrated here by modern artists, show them making use of the opportunity offered by fantasy to alter the relationship of size.

Marija Vogelnik. *Palčica* by H. C. Andersen. Ljubljana, Mladinska Knjiga, 1957

Kaum ist die Hexe aus dem Haus,
kommt Kasperle herein.

Wo mag das Vögelein sein? Er hört sein trauriges
Singen, aber er sieht es nicht. —

Kasperle entdeckt den Käfig unter
dem Hexentuch.
Er holt das Vögelchen aus dem Käfig
heraus. Und dreimal streichelt Kasperle
dem Vögelchen mit der Wunderblume
übers Köpfchen!

Da verwandelt sich das Vögelchen wieder
in Prinzessin Tausendschön!

Kasperle und Tausendschön fallen sich
vor lauter Freude in die Arme.

Kasperle ruft fröhlich aus:
„Nun schnell nach Hause!"

Horst Lemke. *Kasperle und die Wunderblume* by H. M. Denneborg. Ravensburg, Otto Maier, 1963.

Denneborg has given a new lease on life to the Punch and Judy story, whose classic exponent in Germany was Franz Pocci. Both authors are illustrated here by two modern German artists at their best.

Wanda Zacharias. *Kasperls Reise übers Meer* by Franz Pocci. Gütersloh, Sigbert Mohn, 1960.

There are some modern fantasies which are likely to stand beside those of Carroll and Andersen. Among them are those of Tove Jansson who has created two picture-books alongside her more familiar Moomin story-books.

Tove Jansson. *Kuka Lohduttaisi Nyytiä?* Helsinki, Werner Söderstrom, 1960.

Rudolf Moser. *Zötti und Balloni*. Zürich, Atlantis, 1959.

The fantasy of this Swiss picture-book lies more in the manner of its presentation than in the story itself, which is firmly if poetically based in the real world.

He helped the boy scouts learn knots.

Tomi Ungerer. *Crictor*. New York, Harper, 1958.

Violet H. Drummond. *The flying postman.* London, Constable, 1964.

Fantasy here merges with nonsense with the story-tellers' complete acceptance of incongruous situations.

Reiner Zimnik. *Jonas der Angler*.
Munich, 1954; now Berlin, Dressler.

Antony Maitland. *The secret of the shed*. London, Constable, 1962.

LEFT: From one of Zimnik's earliest picture-books, which brought a new talent to children's fantasy.

ABOVE: An example from an English 'mechanical' fairy story.

E. O. Plauen.
Vater und Sohn.
Berlin, Ullstein, 1935.

Picture-Stories

Three examples of one of the most widespread adaptations of the picture-book form; language and print becoming almost entirely redundant.

Hergé. *Le lotus bleu*. A Tintin story. Tournai, Casterman, 1946.

From a picture-story without words published in the Chinese People's Republic c. 1959.

Folding books are known to the German-speaking world as Leporellos because of the way they unfold a catalogue of events. In this they bear an obvious relationship to picture-strips, as in the example below from China where the technique is very popular. Helga Aichinger has adapted the idea in a series of colourful, unconventional books, of which the example shows the stages in the emergence of a butterfly.

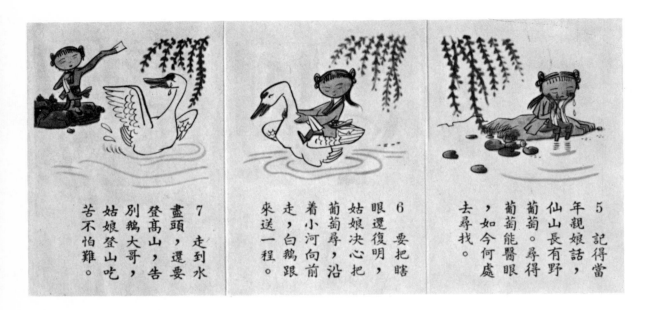

From a Chinese Picture-Story.

Helga Aichinger. *Die Verwandlung des Räupleins*. Lahr, Ernst Kaufmann, 1904.

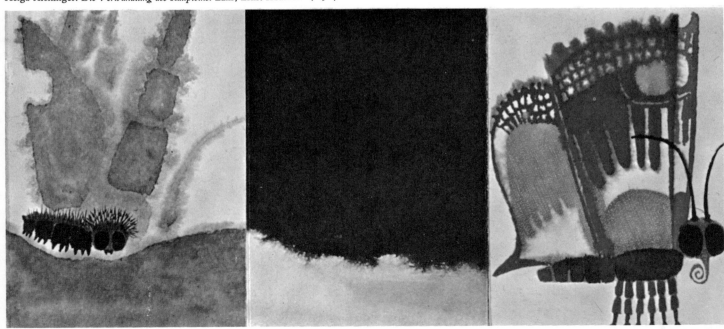

Attempts rather like Lionni's *Little blue and little yellow* are now being made to replace objects and people in picture-books by symbols, language being renounced entirely. The example on this page shows an experimental version of the story of William Tell. On the right is a key to the symbols; below is the scene where Tell and his son approach Gessler's hat. The whole strip is colourfully and intriguingly produced.

Key to the symbols (right):

Wilhelm Tell
Tellenknabe
Landvogt Gessler
Ritter
Saldat
Gesslers Hut
Apfel
Armbrust Pfeil
Bürger
Bürger sich neigend
Zwingburg
Wald
Schiff
Wellen

Warja Honegger-Lavater. *Wilhelm Tell*. Basel, Basilius, 1962.

Lines can be as thin and delicate as a spider web,
or as heavy and black as the bars of a lion's cage.

Lines can be as ragged as a barbed wire fence,
or as smooth as the thread in mother's sewing box.

Helen Borten. *Do you see what I see?* New York, Abelard-Schuman, 1959.

Some picture-books fulfil their purpose by calling on the simplest formal elements either to tell a story, as with Bruna, or to teach something of form itself, as in the two American examples.

Dick Bruna. *Nijntje.*
Utrecht, Bruna, 1963.

daarin woonden twee konijntjes   meneer en mevrouw Pluis

Ann and Paul Rand. *Sparkle and spin.* New York, Harcourt, Brace, 1957.

Sometimes one word sounds
the same as another
like hair and hare
or pair and pear.

The World of Man: Present and Past

Some of the attractions of our modern urban, technical culture to the maker of picture-books.

Virginia Lee Burton. *The little house*. Boston, Houghton Mifflin, 1942.

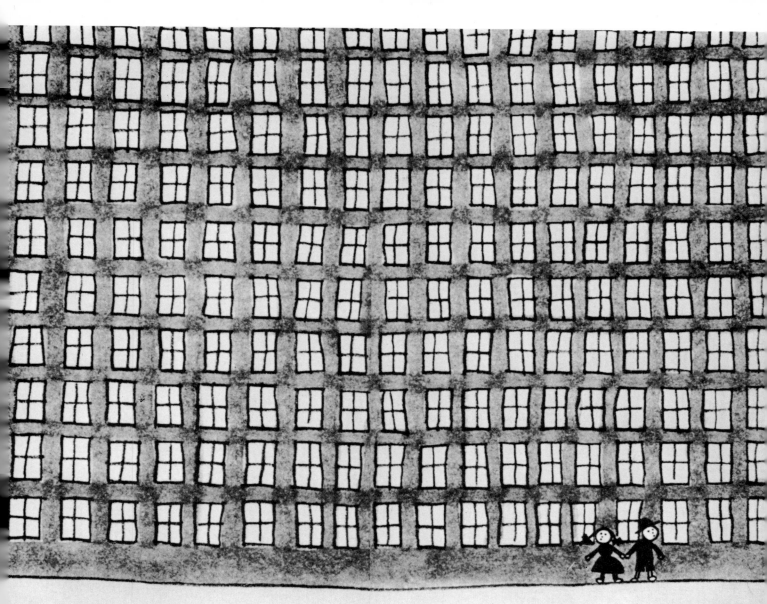

A visit to New York City

Remy Charlip. *A moon or a button* by Ruth Krauss. New York, Harper, 1959.

とりうちぼうしに
ねじりはちまき
みみにはさんだ
みじかい えんぴつ、
こしに つるした
くぎの ふくろ
おじさんたちは、
しごとに はげむ。
「ゆくよ、そら。」
「ほいきた、どっこい。」
しごとが はかどる。
しごとが
すすむ。

Michinori Murata. (*My new house*) Tokyo, Fukuinkan-Shoten, 1960.

A factual account of house-building from Japan.

A dream-house of an American boy which is not as innocent as it looks in this 'exploded' picture.

William Pène du Bois. *Elisabeth the cow ghost*. New York, Viking Press, 1964.

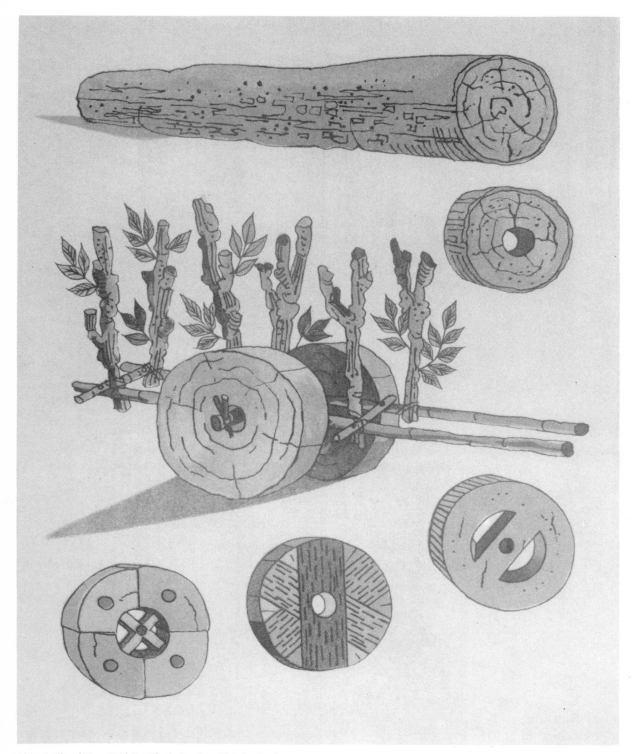

Oliver Hill and Hans Tisdall. *Wheels*. London, Pleiades Books, 1946.

Paxton Chadwick. *Wild animals in Britain*. Harmondsworth, Penguin Books, 1958.

Eileen Mayo. *Animals on the farm*. Harmondsworth, Penguin Books, 1951.

Since the war many English picture-books have been notable for their imaginative and beautifully detailed presentation of factual subjects.

Lewitt-Him. *The little red engine gets a name* by Diana Ross. London, Faber & Faber, 1942.

The age of steam on the railways gave rise to a number of masterpieces in picture-books which (*pace* Ardizzone) the age of Diesel has yet to produce.

Lewitt–Him's *Little Red Engine* (left) is one of the classics among railway picture-books. The same artistic team was also responsible for the first edition of Tuwim's picture-book, more recently illustrated by Lenica (below).

Jan Lenica. *Lokomotywa* by Julian Tuwim. Warsaw, Wydawnictwo 'Polonia', 1958.

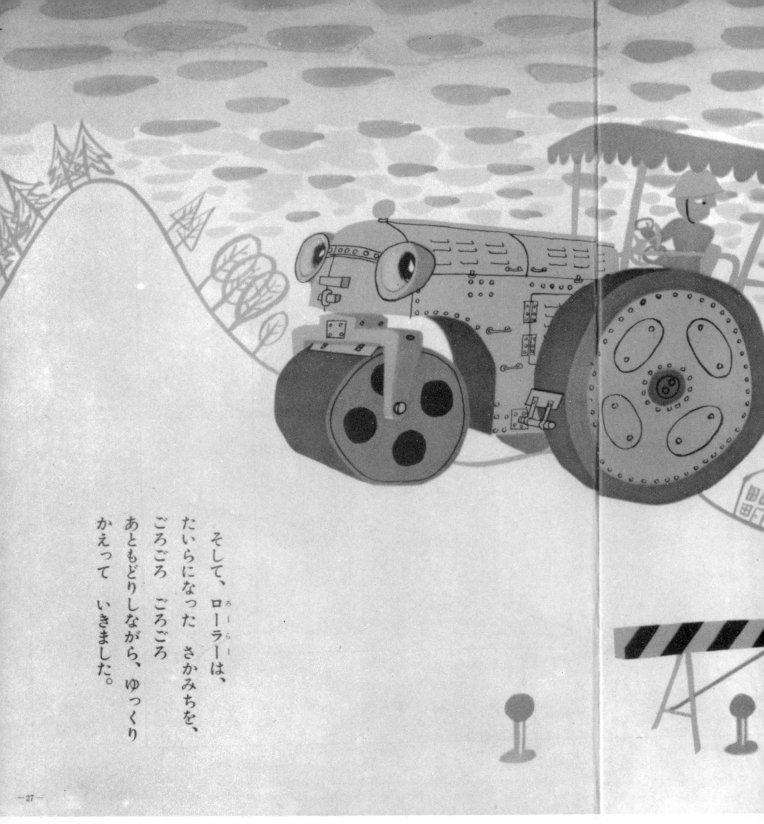

そして、ローラーは、
たいらになった さかみちを、
ごろごろ ごろごろ
あともどりしながら、ゆっくり
かえって いきました。

—27—

Tadayoshi Yamamoto. (*Mr. Slowcoach*) Tokyo, Fukuinkan-Shoten, 1960.

188

A mechanical version of 'the hare and the tortoise' from Japan.

Józef Wilkoń. *Der Kranich mit dem einen Bein* by Paul Schaaf. Cologne, Middelhauve, 1963.

rosa para prepararse dignamente. Ocho días antes de llegar la fiesta comenzaría el rey, junto con la nobleza, a ayunar. También el pueblo tenía que hacerlo, con lo que la vida de Méjico se tornaba un poco más lenta y callada. Y Achitomelt pensó que en estos días se presentaba, mejor que en ningún otro, la deseada oportunidad.

El rey, que durante el resto del tiempo apenas si abandonaba su palacio y cuando lo hacía era precedido por pregoneros que le iban anunciando, salía en los días de ayuno

28

J. A. Sánchez Prieto and Antonio Cuni. *Leyendas Mexicanas* by R. Morales. Madrid, Aguilar, 1958.

ABOVE: The powerful evocation of the Spanish colonial past in a Mexican legend.

LEFT: Some medieval apparatus as the background to a fairy-tale.

Ingri and Edgar Parin d'Aulaire. *Benjamin Franklin*. New York, Doubleday, 1950.

ABOVE: A vivid pictorial account of one of the most hackneyed themes in American scientific lore.

RIGHT: A dream-visit to America's more distant past.

Berta and Elmer Hader.
*Little Antelope,
an Indian for a day.*
New York,
Macmillan, 1962.

A theatrical setting for a picture-book on the legendary past.

Suekichi Akaba. Illustration for a Japanese legend. Tokyo, Fukuinkan-Shoten, 1961.

Les hommes chassaient le phoque, le morse, l'oumka-
ours-blanc. Après la chasse, ils jouaient ensemble,
à des jeux de force, d'adresse. Alors Oulgoun, le
graveur sur l'os, prenait une dent de morse. En
dessinant dessus, il racontait la chasse, les jeux, tout
ce qu'il voyait. Les gens riaient de plaisir en le regar-
dant. Parce que les dessins d'Oulgoun les montraient
si forts, si braves, si heureux.

René Moreu. *La montagne du souriceau* by Luda Schnitzer. Paris, Flammarion, 1963.

The birth of legend itself—tribal events being recorded in picture-language
on a piece of whalebone.

Susanne Ehmcke. *Der Reimallein*. Freiburg, Atlantis, 1964.

An appropriate conclusion; but perhaps a question mark should be added. Does the picture-book world repay all this serious consideration? Does it have any influence on the perceptions of children who enter it? Will it be able to withstand the pressures of the mass-media, and especially television and new developments in photography and cinema? It is perhaps worth thinking about these matters while we are blessed with so many fine examples and while so many serious artists are devoting the best of their talents to picture-books for children.

Translator's Note

In translating the first section of this book I have adhered fairly closely to Mrs. Hürlimann's original text but have, with her permission, slightly altered the emphases in one or two chapters and rewritten parts of the chapters on English and American picture-books. I have also tried to include full publication details of books not referred to anywhere else in the text. The notes in the Illustrations Section have been extensively revised in consultation with Mrs. Hürlimann, who was anxious that comparative details should be more fully stressed.

Much of my attention has been devoted to expanding Mrs. Waldmann's bio-bibliographical supplement, bearing in mind the special needs of English and American readers. Considering the importance of picture-books in the child's experience it is astonishing that so little systematic attention has been paid to them or to the artists who created them. Few books (of which the two Horn Book volumes are the most comprehensive) have been devoted entirely to picture-books and even fewer to the work of individual illustrators. Despite the fact that artists are usually more influential than authors at this stage of a child's reading, they often do not receive individual mention in bibliographies, or even in many indexes to book-lists or general surveys of the literature.

Because of this dearth of proper attention to the subject I have made some attempt to set an example in my expansions of Mrs. Waldmann's bibliographical notes. At the risk of appearing pedantic I have given most of the information that appeared in the German edition and have added details of American and English publications where I felt it to be necessary. It would have been instructive to have included complete artist bibliographies in all cases, but this presents enormous problems with foreign artists and with such prolific workers as Ardizzone, or Duvoisin, or Rojankovsky. As it is, where bibliographies are given, I have tried to include the artists' first and their most recent books, with a list of significant or outstanding specimens in between. At the same time I have appended a note of sources of further information if such exist. This will have served a good purpose if it does nothing more than acknowledge the many debts which we owe to the bibliographical work of Horn Book Inc. of Boston. It is unfortunate that so few libraries in England possess even an approximation to a complete run of the *Horn Book Magazine*.

Acknowledgements

For advice and encouragement as this translation has proceeded I am greatly indebted to Miss Eva Berg and to my colleague Miss Eleanor von Schweinitz. The resources of the Hertfordshire County Library have been made freely available to me in the bibliographical checking which I have undertaken and Miss Susan Jones has been especially helpful in rounding up elusive bits of information. I have also made use of the catalogue of children's book illustrators at the Holborn Central Library. This seems to be the only attempt in a British library to keep up with the work of illustrators of both picture-books and children's novels, and it deserves every encouragement for its enterprise. My wife has again undertaken the unenviable task of typing a heavily revised manuscript and has complained less than I deserve at my prolonged abstentions from family affairs.

B. W. A.

Bio-Bibliographical Supplement

In quoting sources of further information I have relied heavily on a few biographical surveys and reviewing journals. Full publication details of these are given in the general bibliography at the end of the book; the following are short-title references:

Mahony. *Illustrators of children's books, 1744–1945*. Viguers. *Illustrators of children's books, 1946–1956*. Caldecott (1). *Caldecott Medal books, 1938–1957*. Caldecott (2). *Newbery and Caldecott Medal books, 1956–1965*. Kunitz & Haycraft. *The junior book of authors*. Fuller. *More junior authors*. HB. *Horn Book Magazine*. JB. *Junior bookshelf*. CBN. *Children's book news*. Ryder. *Artists of a certain line*.

AAS, Tonje Strøm. Born 1937, lives in Norway; 1954–59 student at the school of industrial design in Oslo. 1959 married the sculptor Nils Aas and has a young son. She illustrates texts for reading books and in 1960, 1961, and 1963 she gained prizes from the Norwegian Ministry of Education for her work in this field. (p. 96)

ADAMS, Adrienne. Born in Arkansas; studied at the University of Missouri and the American School of Design. After a spell of teaching she worked as a free-lance commercial artist. Her book illustrations show a complete command of the delicate effects which can be achieved in lithographic work.

Gordon, P. *The 13th is magic*. Lothrop, 1950. Godden, R. *Impunity Jane*. Viking, 1954; Macmillan, 1955. Goudey, A. E. *Houses from the sea*. Scribner, 1959. Fisher, A. *Going barefoot*. Crowell, 1960. Grimm, J. and W. *The shoemaker and the elves*. Scribner, 1960. Andersen, H. C. *Thumbelina*. Scribner, 1961. *Bring a torch Jeannette Isabella*. Scribner, 1963. Haviland, V. *Favourite fairy tales told in Scotland*. Little, 1963; Bodley, 1966. Goudey, A. E. *Butterfly time*. Scribner, 1964. Grimm, J. and W. *Snow White and Rose Red*. Scribner, 1964. Fisher, A. *In the middle of the night*. Crowell, 1965. Wahl, J. *Cabbage moon*. Holt, 1965. Andersen, H. C. *The ugly duckling*. Scribner, 1966. Lang, A. *The twelve dancing princesses*. Holt, 1966.
BIOG. Viguers, 62.
BID. Viguers, 209.

AICHINGER, Helga. Born 1937 in Linz, where she still lives; attended the Linz College of Art. Her first book, *Der Rattenfänger*, made use of techniques of paper-tearing and received first prize at the Brussels World Fair. Since then she has illustrated fairy tales (including a German translation of *Little grey men*) and popular folding-books. (p. 176)

Der Rattenfänger. Neugebauer, 1963. *Die bunte Märchentruhe*. Trauner, 1963. *Die Verwandlung des Räupleins*. Kaufmann, 1964. (And other folding-books.) *Der Hirt*. Middelhauve, 1966. Translated as *The Shepherd*. Dobson, 1966; Crowell, 1967. *Der Elefant, die Maus und der Floh*. Middelhauve, 1966. Translated as *The elephant, the mouse and the flea*. Faber; Atheneum, 1967.

AKABA, Suekichi. Born 1910 in Tokyo, lives in Japan; self taught. After travels in Manchuria and Inner Mongolia he began to paint pictures to illustrate old Japanese legends and fairy tales, chiefly for the pleasure of his six children, three of whom were killed during the war. This tragic loss has committed him more than ever to his work on picture-books. (p. 194)

AMBRUS, Victor G. Born 1935 in Budapest, the son of a chemical engineer; studied graphic design at the Hungarian Academy of Fine Art. In 1956 he was involved in the Hungarian uprising and later escaped and made his way to England. He studied engraving and lithography at the Royal College of Art and was a 'Royal Scholar' there in 1958. On leaving he worked for a studio in London, but is now a free-lance artist and teacher of illustration and drawing. His early colour books reflected his keen enthusiasm for military history (he likes to collect old weapons, particularly swords), but in 1965 he produced his first picture-story book, *The three poor tailors*, an adaptation of a Hungarian folk-tale. In this year, too, he was awarded the Kate Greenaway Medal.

Dawlish, P. *The Royal Navy*. O.U.P., 1963. Fitzgerald, E. *The British Army*. O.U.P., 1964. Taylor, J. W. R. *The Royal Air Force*. O.U.P., 1965. *The three poor tailors*. O.U.P., 1965; Harcourt, 1966. Dawlish, P. *The Merchant Navy*. O.U.P., 1966. *Brave soldier Janosh*. O.U.P.; Harcourt, 1967.
BIB. JB (March 1964).
BIOG. JB (June 1966) by the artist himself.
CRIT. JB (March 1964) by M. R. Hodgkin.

ARDIZZONE, Edward. Born 1900 in Indo-China, lives in London; attended evening classes in drawing while working as a clerk, and at the age of twenty-six he turned successfully to freelance painting. He has illustrated more than a hundred books, both for adults and children, his earliest ones being done for his own children and showing his close attachment to the sea and the details of English life. In 1956 he became the first recipient of the Kate Greenaway Medal for *Tim all alone*. (p. 112)

Little Tim and the brave sea captain. O.U.P., 1936; 2nd edn, O.U.P.; Walck, 1955. *Lucy Brown and Mr. Grimes*. O.U.P., 1936. *Tim and Lucy go to sea*. O.U.P., 1938; 2nd edn, O.U.P.; Walck, 1958. de la Mare. *Peacock pie*. Faber, 1946; Knopf, 1961. *Nicholas and the fast-moving diesel*. Eyre & Spottiswoode, 1948; 2nd edn, O.U.P.; Walck, 1959. *Paul the hero of the fire*. Penguin, 1948; Houghton, 1949; 2nd edn, Constable, 1962; Walck, 1963. *Tim to the rescue*. O.U.P.; Walck, 1949. Reeves, J. *The blackbird in the lilac*. O.U.P., 1952; Dutton, 1959. Reeves, J. *The exploits of Don Quixote*. Blackie, 1959; Walck, 1960. Reeves, J. *Titus in trouble*. Bodley, 1959; Walck, 1960. Graves, R. *The penny fiddle*. Cassell, 1960; Doubleday, 1961. Barrie, J. M. *Peter Pan*. Brockhampton, 1962. Farjeon, E. *Mrs. Malone*. O.U.P.; Walck, 1962. Reeves, J. *Three tall tales*. Abelard, 1964. Reeves, J. *The Story of Jackie Thimble*. Chatto, 1965. Ross, D. *Old Perisher*. Faber, 1965. *Tim and Ginger*. O.U.P.; Walck, 1965. *The little girl and the tiny doll*. Delacorte, 1961; Constable, 1966.
BIB. Mahony, 386; Viguers, 210.
BIOG. Viguers, 64–65; JB (March 1950) by the artist himself; Fuller 2; Ryder, 44–45.
CRIT. HB (May 1950) by Helen Stone; *Motif* (November 1958 and February 1959) by Ardizzone and Lynton Lamb.

AYER, Jacqueline. Studied in New York and Paris. On her marriage she moved to Thailand and observed carefully the varied way of life there. Her picture-books attempt to show that although children may differ in the colour of their skins or the clothes they wear, they are very similar in the way they think and feel. (p. 133)

Nu Dang and his kite. Harcourt, 1959; Collins, 1960. *A wish for little sister*, Harcourt, 1960; Collins, 1961. *The paper flower tree*. Harcourt, 1962; Collins, 1963. Yershov, P. *Humpy*. Harcourt, 1966.

BEMELMANS, Ludwig. Born 1898 in Merano, died 1962. Son of a Belgian painter; arrived in the U.S.A. at the age of sixteen and worked in hotels while he learned painting. A mural which he painted for a restaurant attracted the attention of the New York publishers Viking, by whom he was encouraged to create his first book: *Hansi* (1934). He became famous for his *Madeline* books which mingled experiences of his own, impressions of Paris, and events in the life of his daughter. In 1954 he received the Caldecott Medal for *Madeline's rescue*. (p. 138)

Hansi. Viking, 1934. *The golden basket*. Viking, 1936. *Quito express*. Viking, 1938; 1965. *Madeline*. Simon, 1939; Deutsch, 1952. *Madeline's rescue*. Viking; Deutsch, 1953. *Parsley*. Harper, 1955. *Madeline and the bad hat*. Viking, 1957; Deutsch, 1958. *Madeline and the gypsies*. Viking, 1959; Deutsch, 1961. *Welcome home!* Harper, 1960. *Madeline in London*. Viking, 1961; Deutsch, 1962.
BIB. Mahony, 388; Viguers, 212.
BIOG. Viguers, 72–73; Caldecott (1) by M. Massee; JB (December 1954); Fuller, 14–15; and volumes of autobiography.

BENNETT, Rainey. Born 1907 in Marion, Indiana; lives in Chicago; trained at various art schools. He works in advertising, paints murals, and has been illustrating books since 1931. He is famous for his water-colours, which have arisen out of his travels. They are to be seen in the big American galleries and have influenced the style of his delicate and sensitive illustrations for children. (p. 70)

What do you think? 1958. *The secret hiding place*, 1960; Blackie, 1964. *After the sun goes down*, 1961. (All World Pub. Co.)
CRIT. HB (October 1962) by Adrienne Adams.

BERKOVÁ, Dagmar. Born 1920, lives in Czechoslovakia. Has illustrated books by Czechoslovakian and foreign authors, including Carroll's *Alice* books (p. 164) and E. T. A. Hoffmann's *Nussknacker und Mäusekönig*.

BETTINA (i.e. Bettina Ehrlich). Born 1903 in Vienna, lives in London. She spent her childhood at Vienna and Grado, an island in the Adriatic. She spent some time at the Vienna School of Industrial Design where she learnt lithography and printed two picture-books by hand. In 1930 she married the sculptor Georg Ehrlich, and in 1938 they moved to London. She has been working on picture-books since 1942, and many of them have their setting in the Adriatic landscapes of her youth. (p. 139)

Poo-Tsee, the water tortoise. Chatto, 1943. *Carmello*. Chatto, 1945. *Cocolo*. Chatto, 1945; Harper, 1948. *A horse for the island*. Harper, 1952; Hamilton, 1953. Kingman, L. *The magic Christmas tree*. Farrar, 1956; O.U.P., 1957. *Angelo and Rosaline*. Collins, 1957. *Pantaloni*. Harper, 1957; O.U.P., 1959. *Trovato*. Farrar, 1959; O.U.P., 1960. Hosier, J. *The sorcerer's apprentice*. O.U.P., 1960; Walck, 1961. *Dolls*. O.U.P., 1962; Farrar, 1963. *Francesco and Francesca*. O.U.P., 1962. *Of uncles and aunts*. O.U.P., 1963; Norton, 1964. *Goat boy*. O.U.P., 1965; Norton, 1966. *Paolo and Panetto*. O.U.P.; Watts, 1960. *Sardines and the angel*. O.U.P., 1967.
BIB. Viguers, 213.
BIOG. Viguers, 74; Fuller, 16–17.
CRIT. HB (October 1952) by the artist herself.

BISCHOFF, Helmut: *see under* Winter, Klaus.

BIZOVIČAR, Milan. Born 1927 in Ljubljana, lives in Yugoslavia where he finished his studies in 1951. Since then he has illustrated children's books by various authors and is a regular contributor to two Yugoslavian magazines for young people. (p. 56)

BOBRI, Vladimir (i.e. Vladimir Bobritsky). Born 1898 in Kharkov in the Ukraine, lives in America; art-training in Russia. He fled from the Revolution with a group of gipsy musicians, spent some time painting icons in a Greek monastery and then earned the money for his passage to America by designing costumes and scenery for the Russian ballet in Constantinople. In 1921 he opened a textile-printing business in the U.S.A. and also worked as an advertising artist. He has command of a variety of techniques for his illustrations for children's books. (colour, p. 17)

Beale, W. *Binky*. Lothrop, 1954. Budney, B. *A kiss is round*. Lothrop, 1954. Rice, I. *The march wind*. Lothrop, 1957; World's Work, 1960. Zolotow, C. *The sleepy book*. Lothrop, 1958; World's Work, 1960. Branley, F. M. *What the moon is like*. Crowell, 1963; Black, 1964. Slobodkin, E. *Boris and his balalaika*. Abelard, 1965. Gans, R. *Icebergs*. Crowell, 1964; Black, 1965
BIB. Viguers, 214.
BIOG. Mahony, 279; Viguers, 78; *The American Artist* (March 1942) by E. W. Watson.

BORTEN, Helen. Lives in Pennsylvania; attended art school for four years. She has been an advertising artist and has illustrated books for adults and children. Some of her books attempt through both text and pictures to introduce young children to art and music. (pp. 136 and 178)

Longstreth, J. *Little Big-feather*. Abelard, 1956. *Do you see what I see?* Abelard, 1959. *Do you hear what I hear?* Abelard, 1960. *Do you move as I move?* Abelard, 1963. Branley, F. M. *The sun: our nearest star*. Crowell, 1961; Black, 1963. (And other books in the 'Let's read and find out' series.)

BRAUN-FOCK, Beatrice. Born in Amsterdam, lives in Germany; attended school in Holland and Germany and received artistic training at Munich. During her student years she became the first woman contributor to the *Simplizissimus*. In 1919 her first picture-book appeared with a text by Anatole France: *Bienchen* published by Musarion at Munich; since then she has illustrated books by Paul Alverdes, James Krüss and many other well-known writers. (p. 113)

Heimeran, E. *Der schwarze Schimmel*. Lentz/Betz, 1956. Translated as *Paint a black horse*. Methuen, 1958. Alverdes, P. *Die Traumpferdchen*. Herold, 1957. Krüss, J. *ABC, ABC, Arche Noah sticht in See*. Obpacher, 1959. Alverdes, P. *Vom dicken, fetten Pfannkuchen*. Stalling, 1960.

BRIGGS, Raymond. Born in London in 1934, the son of a south London milkman; studied at the Wimbledon School of Art and the Slade School before turning to writing and illustrating children's books in 1957.

He has written several books for young children and illustrated many more, but he is best known for his richly illustrated selections of traditional rhymes. For the most recent of these, *The Mother Goose treasury*, he was awarded the 1966 Kate Greenaway Medal. He is now working on his own series of books in which he will illustrate stirring achievements by men of courage.

He is married to an artist and lives in Hassocks, Sussex.

Ring-a-ring o' roses, 1962. *The white land*, 1963. *Fee fi fo fum*, 1964. *The Mother Goose treasury*, 1966. (All Hamilton and Coward McCann.)
BIOG. Ryder, 50–51.

BROWN, Marcia. Born 1918 in Rochester, New York; lives in Manhattan. After a number of years of wide study, including a course at the Woodstock School of Painting, she spent some time working in the New York Public Library where she developed her interests in story-telling and puppetry. She has twice been awarded the Caldecott Medal: in 1955 for *Cinderella* and in 1962 for *Once a mouse . . .*

The little carousel, 1946. *Stone soup*, 1947. *Henry, fisherman*, 1949. *Dick Whittington and his cat*, 1950. Perrault, C. *Puss in boots*, 1952. Andersen, H. C. *Steadfast tin soldier*, 1953. Perrault, C. *Cinderella*, 1954. *The flying carpet*, 1956. *Felice*, 1958. *Once a mouse . . .*, 1961. Andersen, H. C. *The wild swans*, 1963. *The backbone of the king*, 1966. *The neighbours*, 1967. (All Scribner.)
BIOG. Viguers, 81; Fuller, 32–33; Caldecott (1) by Alice Dalgliesh; Caldecott (2) by H. A. Masten.
BIB. Viguers, 215.
CRIT. HB (September 1949). *Distinction in picture-books*. HB (June 1967). *My goals as an illustrator*.

BRUNA, Dick. Born 1927 in Utrecht, lives in Holland; self-taught; has designed around 1,000 book jackets and countless advertisements. His very personal style is seen most clearly in his many picture-books, whose simplicity has led to a widespread popularity, not just in Holland but also in England, Germany, Italy, America, and South Africa. (p. 179)

The little bird. Methuen, 1959; U.S. title, *Little bird Tweet*, Follett, 1963. (And many other little picture-books including the *Miffy* books and some simple fairy stories: *Snow White*, 1967, and *Red Riding Hood*, 1967.) *The Christmas book*. Methuen, 1964. *B is for bear*, Methuen, 1967.
BIB. JB (August 1967) by J. Dohm.

BURNINGHAM, John. Born 1936 in Farnham, lives in London. As a conscientious objector he worked out his military service as a civilian in South Italy and Israel. After the war he attended art school and again stayed in Italy as a film designer. He became known in England through his poster designs and his first picture-book, *Borka*, gained for him the 1963 Kate Greenaway Award (p. 108). In addition to picture-books he has designed a series of decorative nursery friezes.

Borka. Cape, 1963; Random, 1964. *ABC*. Cape, 1964; Bobbs, 1967. *Trubloff*. Cape, 1964; Random, 1965. Fleming, I. *Chitty-chitty-bang-bang*. Cape; Random, 1964. *Humbert, Mr. Firkin and the Lord Mayor of London*. Cape, 1965; Bobbs, 1967. *Cannonball Simp*. Cape, 1966; Bobbs, 1967. *Harquin*. Cape, 1967.
CRIT. JB (July 1964). A note by the artist.

BURTON, Virginia Lee. Born 1909 in Massachusetts where she now lives. She studied both dancing and painting and finally turned entirely to the latter. Her first picture-book illustrations could not find a publisher but she later achieved widespread success and was awarded the 1943 Caldecott Medal for *The little house*. (p. 180)

Choo Choo. Houghton, 1937; Faber, 1944. *Mike Mulligan and his steam shovel*. Houghton, 1939; Faber, 1942. *Calico the wonder horse*. Houghton, 1941; Faber, 1942. *The little house*. Houghton, 1942; Faber, 1946. *Katy and the big snow*. Houghton, 1943; Faber, 1947. Malcolmson, A. *The song of Robin Hood*. Houghton, 1947.
BIB. Mahony, 397; Viguers, 216.
BIOG. Viguers, 85; Caldecott (1) by G. A. Hogarth; Kunitz, 62.

CANDEA, Romulus. Born 1922 in Rumania, lives in Vienna where he also received his artistic training. He has been active as a graphic artist with various magazines and publishers and has received many honours in Austria. (p. 15)

Ginzkey, F. K. *Der Träumerhansl*. Jungbrunnen, 1952. Ferra-Mikura, V. *Der alte und der junge und der kleine Stanislaus*. Jungbrunnen, 1962. Translated as *The voyagers*. Sadler and Brown, 1966. Ferra-Mikura, V. *Lustig singt die Regentonne*. Jungbrunnen, 1964.

CARIGIET, Alois. Born 1902 in Truns; son of an alpine farmer; lives in Switzerland. He completed a course as a scene-painter and became a commercial artist. He produced many posters and magazine covers, designed settings for the Zürich cabaret *Cornichon*, travelled about a good deal and executed many murals. He became a children's book illustrator through Selina Chönz whose lyrical Romansh poetry awoke in him a nostalgia for his childhood and who inspired him to recreate his feelings in the pages of a child's picture-book. Six years passed before *Schellen-Ursli* brought to children who spoke not only Romansh but also German, English, French, and Japanese 'something of the light and shimmer of a mountain childhood'. In 1948 its author and illustrator both shared the annual *Schweizerische Jugendbuchpreis* with Hans Fischer. Carigiet has also illustrated reading books for Zürich schools and a volume of fairy tales from Grisons. (p. 124) In 1966 he became the first recipient of the Hans Christian Andersen Medal for illustrators.

Chönz, S. *Schellen-Ursli*. Schweizer Spiegel, 1945. Chönz, S. *Flurina und das Wildvöglein*. Schweizer Spiegel, 1952. Chönz, S. *Der grosse Schnee*. Schweizer Spiegel, 1955. Translated as *A bell for Ursli* (1950), *Florina and the wild bird* (1952) and *The snowstorm* (1961). (All O.U.P. and Walck.) *Zottel, Zick und Zwerg*. Schweizer Spiegel, 1965. Translated as *Anton the goatherd*. Walck, 1966. *Birnbaum, Birke, Berberitze*. Schweizer Spiegel, 1967. Translated as *The pear tree, the birch tree and the barberry bush*. Walck, 1967.
BIOG. Spescha, H. *Alois Carigiet*. Rascher, 1963.
CRIT. HB (March 1951) by M. Simont; *Graphis* (1954–55); HB (February 1960) by K. Werth.

CARLONI, Giancarlo. Born 1941 in Urbino, lives in Milan; studied at Urbino Academy of Art. He has worked on cartoons and, since 1961, on advertising and·television films. This experience is reflected in his work as an illustrator of children's books. (pp. 77 and 123)

Rocca, G. *Il fagiano Gaetano*. Mursia, 1961. Translated as *Gaetano the pheasant*. Harper, 1966. Rodari, G. *Gip nel televisore*. Mursia, 1962.

CHADWICK, Paxton. Born 1903 in Fallowfield, Lancashire, died 1961. A freelance artist who worked in such fields as poster and textile design and cartooning. As a book illustrator he was pre-eminent in subjects connected with natural history, and was commissioned to prepare a group of elegant educational books on this subject. (p. 185)

Gorvett, J. *Wild flowers*. Penguin, 1949. *Pond life*. Penguin, 1952. *Wild animals in Britain*. Penguin, 1958. Harland, W. B. *The earth*. Vista, 1960; Watts, 1960. *Naturescope* and *Pantoscope* series. Cassell, 1960–62.

CHARLIP, Remy. Born 1929 in Brooklyn, lives in New York. He is not only a dancer and designer but also designs stage-sets, costumes, textiles, and carpets. He writes articles and criticism on dancing and teaches drawing to children. It is perhaps this varied activity which enables him to make his picture-books so attractive. (p. 181)

Dress up and let's have a party. Scott, 1956. *Where is everybody?* Scott, 1957; Scholastic Book Services, 1966. Miles, B. *What is the world?* Knopf, 1958. Krauss, R. *A moon or a button*. Harper, 1959.
BIB. Viguers, 217.
BIOG. Viguers, 90.

CHARLOT, Jean. Born 1898 in Paris, lives in Hawaii. He is of mixed descent—French, Russian, Mexican—but grew up in Paris and fought for France in the First World War. He moved to Mexico in 1921 where he made a detailed study of the Maya frescoes and himself took up work on murals. In 1929 he moved to the U.S.A., but continued to visit Mexico regularly and helped to raise the status of the graphic arts there. He has taught at several American universities and has produced murals and paintings in the U.S.A.; he has also published books about Mexican art. As a book illustrator his artistic versatility is clearly shown in his illustrations for various books for children. (p. 117)

Ferrer, M. G. *Tito's hats.* Garden City, 1940. Brown, M. W. *A child's good night book.* Scott, 1943. Brown, M. W. *Two little trains.* Scott, 1949; World's Work, 1960. Schlein, M. *When will the world be mine?* Scott, 1953.
BIB. Mahony, 398; Viguers, 217.
BIOG. Viguers, 90; Fuller, 43.
CRIT. HB (August 1955) by M. Sendak.

CHEVALLIER, Micheline. Born 1930, lives in France; a self-taught artist with a natural feeling for colour and form. Her marriage to a designer of stories in pictures led her to create illustrations for children's books. (p. 132)

Bosco, M. *Babagi et le roi Patap. Yo, le petit Tibétain.* 1962. Daudet, A. *La chèvre de Monsieur Seguin,* 1967. (All Hatier.)

CLAUDE-LAFONTAINE, Pascale. Born 1928, lives in France. She is a fine musician with a predilection for painting and drawing. As the wife of a publisher and the mother of three children it is not surprising that she turned to book illustration. (p. 134)

Saint Blanquat, H. de. *La fille au sourire. Gulliver à Liliput.* Both Hatier, 1962. Lefébure, A.-M. *Romain l'étourdi.* Tisné, 1967.

COONEY, Barbara. Born 1917 in Brooklyn, lives in Massachusetts; after leaving school she took a course in etching and lithography. She has worked for periodicals and has illustrated texts by a varied group of authors and by herself. She tends to base her pictures on things which she knows very well or which she is able to copy from life. She received the 1959 Caldecott Medal for *Chanticleer and the fox.* (p. 148)

Malmberg, B. *Åke and his world.* Farrar, 1940. Krasilovsky, P. *The man who didn't wash his dishes.* Doubleday, 1950; World's Work, 1962. Kingman, L. *Peter's long walk.* Doubleday, 1953. *Chanticleer and the fox.* Crowell, 1958; Constable, 1960. Otto, M. G. *The little brown horse.* Holt, 1959; Hamilton, 1965. *The little juggler.* Hastings; Constable, 1961. Jewett, S. O. *A white heron.* Crowell, 1963; Constable, 1964. Haviland, V. *Favourite fairy tales of Spain.* Little, 1963; Bodley, 1966. Latham, H. *Mother Goose in French.* Crowell, 1964; Constable, 1965. *Snow-white and Rose-red.* Constable, 1965; Delacorte, 1966. Molloy, A. *Shaun and the boat.* Hastings; Sadler, 1965. *The courtship of Cock Robin and Jenny Wren.* Scribner, 1965; Sadler, 1966. Morse, S. F. *All in a suitcase.* Little, 1966.
BIB. Mahony, 399; Viguers, 218.
BIOG. Viguers, 93; Caldecott (2) by A. N. Porter; Fuller, 53–54.
CRIT. HB (October 1960) by A. A. Watson; HB (February 1961) by the artist herself.

D'AULAIRE, Edgar and Ingri Parin. Edgar—born 1898 in Switzerland; Ingri—born 1904 in Norway; they live in Connecticut. Edgar is of Huguenot stock and originally worked at book illustration and wall-painting, Ingri originally at child portraiture and landscape painting. They married in 1925 and have lived in the U.S.A. since 1929. Here, with the encouragement of Anne Carroll Moore, the New York children's librarian, they studied together the fundamentals of children's book illustration before producing their own largely factual picture-books which were lithographed by Edgar himself. They have two sons. In 1940 they were awarded the Caldecott Medal for their book on Lincoln. (p. 192)

The magic rug. Doubleday, 1931. *The Lord's prayer.* Doubleday, 1934. *Children of the North Lights.* Viking, 1935; Woodfield, 1960. *George Washington.* Doubleday, 1936. *Abraham Lincoln.* Doubleday, 1939. *Don't count your chicks.* Doubleday, 1943. *Benjamin Franklin.* Doubleday, 1950. *Columbus.* Doubleday, 1955.
BIB. Mahony, 403; Viguers, 220.
BIOG. Viguers, 98–9; Caldecott (1) by B. E. Mahony and M. M. Mitchell; Kunitz, 12–13; HB (September 1935).

DOORNEKAMP, Marijke. Born 1943 in Utrecht, lives in Holland. She is in charge of a kindergarten and illustrates for a children's magazine. The example selected here is from a book of Dutch nursery rhymes. (p. 94)

DRUMMOND, Violet H. Born 1911 in London, where she now lives. From childhood onwards she enjoyed drawing and received some training at the St. Martin's School of Art. She began to create picture-books for her own son, which helps to explain the harmony of text and pictures in her work. Her characters are everyday folk who find themselves in situations which are anything but usual—for all the normality of the surroundings. She was awarded the 1957 Kate Greenaway Medal for *Mrs. Easter and the storks.* (p. 171)

Phewtus the squirrel. O.U.P., 1939; Constable, 1966. *Mrs. Easter's parasol.* Faber, 1944. *Miss Anna Truly.* Faber, 1945; Houghton, 1949; Constable, 1965. *Lady Talavera.* Faber, 1946; 1965. *Tidgie's innings.* Faber, 1947; 1966. *The flying postman.* Penguin, 1948; Houghton, 1949; Constable; Walck, 1964. *Mrs. Easter and the storks.* Faber, 1957; Barnes, 1959. *Little Laura's cat.* Faber, 1960. *Little Laura and the lonely ostrich.* Nelson, 1963. And other *Laura* books.
BIB. Viguers, 103.
BIOG. Viguers, 221; HB (Jan./Feb. 1948) by G. A. Hogarth; JB (October 1949) by M. Crouch.

DU BOIS, William Pène. Born 1916 in Nutley, New Jersey, lives in New York. His childhood, partly spent in France, and his subsequent choice of career were much influenced by frequent visits to circuses and by the artistic preoccupations of both his parents and his grandparents. By the age of twenty he was creating picture-books and he has used this form to embody his comic ideas and his love of all kinds of motive power. (p. 183)

Elisabeth the cow ghost. Viking, 1936. *Three policemen.* Viking, 1938. Ashford, D. *The young visiters.* Doubleday, 1951. Godden, R. *The mousewife.* Viking; Macmillan, 1951. *The bear party.* Viking, 1951. *Lion.* Viking, 1956. *Otto at sea.* Viking, 1958; Brockhampton, 1960. *The three little pigs.* Viking, 1962. Lear, E. *The owl and the pussy-cat.* Doubleday, 1962. Caudill, R. *A certain small shepherd.* Holt, 1965; Oliver & Boyd, 1966.
BIB. Mahony, 405; Viguers, 221.
BIOG. Viguers, 103; Kunitz, 102–4.

DUTKOWSKA, Barbara. Born 1921, lives in Poland; studied art at Warsaw. She has designed posters and has taken part in exhibitions at home and abroad. Her feeling for humour and poetry finds expression in her illustrations for children's books. (p. 125)

DUVOISIN, Roger. Born 1904 in Geneva, lives in the United States; studied art in Switzerland and gained experience designing murals, stage scenery, ceramics, and textiles. Shortly before moving to the United States in the late 1920s he married Louise Fatio and it was for their son that his first children's books were created. He became an American citizen in 1938. He has now illustrated a vast body of work by many authors, not the least prolific being himself, and he received the 1948 Caldecott Medal for *White snow, bright snow*, (p. 20), which arose out of the Great Freeze of the previous winter. The translation into German of Louise Fatio's *The happy lion* was awarded the first *Deutscher Jugendbuchpreis* in 1956. (p. 71)

A little boy was drawing. Scribner, 1932. Browning, R. *Pied piper of Hamelin*. Grosset, 1936. *Mother Goose*. Heritage, 1936. Stevenson, R. L. *A child's garden of verses*. Heritage, 1944. Tresselt, A. *White snow, bright snow*. Lothrop, 1947. *Petunia*. Knopf, 1950; Bodley, 1958 (and other titles in this series). *A for ark*. Lothrop, 1952; Bodley, 1961. Fatio, L. *The happy lion*. Whittlesey, 1954; Bodley, 1955 (and other titles). *House of four seasons*. Lothrop, 1956; Brockhampton, 1960. Martin, P. *The pointed brush*. Lothrop, 1959; World's Work, 1960. *Veronica*. Knopf, 1961; Bodley, 1962 (and other titles in this series). Calhoun, M. *Nine lives of Homer C. Cat*. Morrow, 1961; World's Work, 1963. *The miller, his son and their donkey*. McGraw, 1962; Bodley, 1963. Fatio, L. *Red bantam*. McGraw; Bodley, 1963.
BIB. Mahony, 405; Viguers, 221. Kerlan, I. *A Roger Duvoisin bibliography*. Univ. of Virginia, 1958.
BIOG. Viguers, 103–4; Caldecott (1) by D. Waugh; HB (January 1948); Kunitz, 106–7.
CRIT. HB (April 1959) by N. Unwin.

EFRAT, Michal. Born 1926 in Czechoslovakia and was for four years in a concentration camp. After the war he attended a school of graphic art in Prague and in 1949 he emigrated to Israel where he now lives in a kibbutz. (p. 146)

EHMCKE, Susanne. Born 1906 in Düsseldorf. Lives in Munich; as the daughter of a well-known book artist, Professor Fritz Ehmcke, she found little difficulty in the choice of a career. She studied at Munich, Zürich, and Vienna, and since the early 1930s she has been among the pioneers of the finely designed picture-book. She is also a sensitive writer and this gives her books a special artistic unity. (p. 196)

Vogelbart. Maier, 1943; rev. edn, 1965. *Die Jahreszeiten*. Maier, 1953. *Kinderduden*. Bib. Inst.; Harrap, 1959. *Das kleine rote Auto*. Maier, 1960. *Der Reimallein*. Atlantis, 1964.

FISCHER, Hans. Born 1909 in Berne, died 1958. After attending various art schools he was active as a commercial artist in Berne and from 1937 on he was stage designer for the Zürich *Cornichon* cabaret and also designed murals. He created his first picture-book, *Die Bremer Stadtmusikanten*, for his first child, *Das Lumpengesindel* for the second, and for the third *Der Geburtstag* and *Pitschi*, whose texts he wrote himself. *Der Geburtstag* gained him the *Schweizerische Jugendbuchpreis* in 1948. He also created many murals and illustrations for adult publications, while foreign editions of his picture-books gave him a reputation far beyond Switzerland. Shortly before his death he, like Carigiet, was commissioned to illustrate new schoolbooks for the canton of Zürich. (pp. 160 and 161)

Die Bremer Stadtmusikanten. Artemis, 1944. Translated as *The travelling musicians*. Cassell, 1948; Harcourt, 1955. *Das Lumpengesindel*. Artemis, 1945. *Der Geburtstag*. Artemis, 1947. Translated as *The birthday*. Harcourt, 1954. *Pitschi*. Artemis, 1948. Translated under the same title. Harcourt, 1953. *Rum-pum-pum*. Artemis, 1951. Translated under the same title. Harcourt, 1964. *Der gestiefelte Kater*. Artemis, 1957. Translated as *Puss-in-boots*. Harcourt, 1959; Benn, 1962. (Before 1959 Fischer's books were published by Verlag der Wolfsbergdrucke and Büchergilde Gutenberg.)
BIB. Viguers, 223.

BIOG. Viguers, 110; Fuller, 84; *Graphis* (no. 17, 1958) by A. M. Vogt; Kasser, H. *Hans Fischer genannt Fis*. Zürich, Artemis, 1959.

FONTANA, Ugo. Born 1921 in Florence, lives in Italy. He turned early on to painting and illustrative work for children, notably the picture stories for the periodical *Corriere dei ragazzi*. He also interests himself in theories about picture-books and likes to keep in touch with educationists and psychologists. Among the author whom he has illustrated for children are Andersen, Grimm, Perrault, Tolstoy, Mark Twain, and Stevenson. (p. 35)

Andersen, H. C. *Thumbelina*. Macmillan, N.Y., 1962.

FRANÇOIS, André. Born 1915 in Rumania, lives in France. He spent his childhood in Rumania, Hungary, and France, and studied art in Paris. He has worked as a painter, cartoonist (for *Punch* among others), designer of magazine covers, and book artist. His children's books are distinguished by their imaginative playfulness. (p. 147)

Harris, I. *Little boy Brown*. Lippincott, 1949. Symonds, J. *The magic currant bun*. Lippincott, 1952; Faber, 1953. *Les larmes de crocodile*. Delpire, 1954. Translated as *Crocodile tears*. Faber, 1955; Universe, 1956. Le Marchand, J. *L'odyssée*. Le Prat, 1954. Translated as *The adventures of Ulysses*. Criterion, 1959; Faber, 1960. de l'Anselme, J. *On vous l'a dit?* Delpire, 1955. Symonds, J. *The story George told me*. Harrap, 1963; Pantheon, 1964.
BIB. Viguers, 224.
BIOG. Viguers, 113.

FRANÇOISE (i.e. Françoise Seignobosc). Born 1900 in France, died 1961. She began painting very early on, and when eventually she started to work for a Paris children's book publisher he sent her pictures to the United States. A scholarship enabled her to realize her wish to discuss her work herself with publishers in that country and from that time on she divided her time between America, Paris, and a farm in Southern France. (p. 126)

Gay Mother Goose and *Gay ABC*. Scribner, 1938. *The thank you book*. Scribner, 1947; Brockhampton, 1955. *Jeanne-Marie counts her sheep*. Scribner, 1951; Brockhampton, 1955; and other Jeanne-Marie books. *Minou*. Scribner, 1962; Brockhampton, 1964.
BIB. Mahony, 437; Viguers, 224.
BIOG. Viguers, 113–14; Fuller, 89; *Françoise speaks to the children* in HB (December 1953).

FRASCONI, Antonio. Born 1919 in Montevideo, lives in America; attended art schools in Uruguay and New York. In spite of his success as a painter he has been preoccupied since 1943 with the making and printing of woodcuts in which he portrays working people, farmers, and, time and again, the sun. His childhood was bilingual (parents: Italian, school: Spanish) and this is reflected in his picture-books, which try to give young children an awareness of more languages than their own. (p. 116)

Aesop. *Twelve fables*, Museum of Modern Art, 1954. *See and say*, 1955. *The house that Jack built*, 1958. *The snow and the sun*, 1961. *See again, say again*, 1964. *Sunday in Monterey*, 1964. (All Harcourt.)
BIB. Viguers, 224.
BIOG. Viguers, 114.

FROMM, Lilo. Born 1928 in Berlin where she now spends most of her time; studied art at Freiburg, Munich, and Hamburg. During her student years she supported herself by drawing for newspapers and by commercial art; later she turned increasingly to freelance work, to brightly coloured illustrations for picture-books, and to delicate line-drawings, mostly for books by other authors. In 1961 she gained the *Deutscher Jungendbuchpreis* for *Das Mondgesicht* (p. 13) and in 1967 the same prize for *Der goldene Vogel*.

Wietig, A. *Es liegt was in der Luft*. Ellermann, 1960. Scheidl, M. *Das Mondgesicht*. Obpacher, 1960. Rechlin, E. *Heut wandern wir zum Zoo*. Stalling, 1961. Duchow, C. *Oberpotz und Hoppelhans*. Obpacher, 1962. Bachér, I. *Das Kinderhaus*. Atlantis, 1965. *Pumpernick und Pimpernell*. Ellermann, 1967.

FUKA, Vladimír. Born 1926 in Pisek (Czechoslovakia), lives in Prague. His studies at the national school of graphic art and at the Academy of Pictorial Art in Prague gave him a firm foundation for his fine work as a book-designer and illustrator. He is a typical representative of the contemporary taste which prevails among young artists, and which enjoys almost technical drawings with a satiric edge to them rather than anything more poetic. Nevertheless his illustrations are witty and full of expression. (p. 145)

GALDONE, Paul. Born in Budapest; travelled to the United States at the age of fourteen. After several years of part-time study at The Art Students League he worked for the publishing firm of Doubleday, but his career was interrupted by war service. After the war he became a free-lance illustrator and is notable for his use of line and his feeling for composition on the page. These, together with his abundant humour, are the striking features of his picture-books.

Taylor, M. *Did you feed my cow?* Crowell, 1956. Titus, E. *Anatole*. Whittlesey, 1956; Bodley, 1957 (and other titles). *Old Mother Hubbard*. McGraw, 1960; Bodley, 1961. *The old woman and her pig*. McGraw; Bodley, 1960. *The house that Jack built*. McGraw, 1961; Bodley, 1962. Jacobs, J. *The three wishes*. McGraw, 1961; World's Work, 1963. Lear, E. *Two old bachelors*. McGraw, 1962; Bodley, 1963. *Shadrach, Meshach and Abednego*. McGraw, 1965. Buckley, H. *The little boy and the birthdays*. Lothrop, 1965. Showers, P. *Your skin and mine*. Crowell, 1965; Black, 1966. Lear, E. *Two laughable lyrics*. Putnam, 1966. *The history of Simple Simon*. McGraw; Bodley, 1966.
BIOG. Viguers, 116–17.
BIB. Viguers, 225.

GAUGUIN, Paul René. Born 1911 in Copenhagen, lives in Norway; although he is a grandson of the French Paul Gauguin he is described as a Danish artist. He works chiefly in colour woodcuts and although he has produced little as an illustrator of children's books, his *Lille Persille* (with text by Inger Hagerup) was awarded the Norwegian prize for picture-books. (p. 95)

GITZ-JOHANSEN, Aáge. Born 1897 in Odense, which was also the birthplace of Hans Christian Andersen; received his training in Copenhagen. His most famous book about Gaba, the Greenlander, was inspired by several journeys in that country. (p. 135)

GOÑI, Lorenzo. Born 1911 in Jaén, Spain, lives in Madrid; up till 1939 he worked as a painter, graphic artist, and draughtsman in Barcelona. From the age of five he has been deaf, but despite the isolation in which this placed him he has produced illustrations for more than 150 books of a high literary standard. His illustrations for Sánchez-Silva's *Marcelino* volumes have been well received abroad as well as in Spain. (p. 37)

Sánchez-Silva, J. M. *Marcelino*. Aguilar, 1952. Translated under the same title, Brown & Nolan, 1954.

GOŠNIK-GODEK, Ančka. Born 1927 in Celje, Yugoslavia and still lives in that country; has illustrated chiefly fairy stories—Per-rault, traditional Slovene tales, and tales by modern Yugoslavian authors. (p. 130)

GRABIAŃSKI, Janusz. Born 1929 in Poland where he still lives; studied art in Kraków and Warsaw. As a painter his preferences are for water-colours as a medium and animals as a subject. He has been awarded numerous prizes and his volumes of animal tales and fairy tales have been published in England and Germany. (p. 121)

Konopnicka, M. *Fränzchen*. Kinderbuchverlag, 1958. *Frohes Singen, frohes Klingen*. Uberreuter, 1960. Grimm, J. and W. *Fairy tales*. Cape; Duell, 1962. Andersen, H. *Fairy tales*. Cape; Duell, 1963. *The Arabian nights*. Cape; Duell, 1964. *The big book of wild animals*. Dobson; Watts, 1964. *The big book of animal stories*. Dobson; Watts, 1965. *Grabiański's cats* and *Grabiański's horses*. Both Dent, 1967.

GRIEDER, Walter. Born 1914 in Basel, where he now lives. After a turbulent Bohemian youth in France, he attended two schools of industrial design in Switzerland, to be followed by a number of years devoted to thinking, writing, and painting. He spent some time studying in Paris and working in a London advertising agency, then in 1957 he opened his own studio of graphic art in Basel. His first picture-book appeared in 1961. (colour illus., p. 45)

Die Geburtstagsreise. Herder, 1961. *Das verzauberte Schloss*. Herder, 1965. *Pierrot und seine Freunde im Zirkus*. Maier, 1965. Translated as *Pierrot*. Seymour Lawrence, 1967. *Das grosse Fest*. Herder, 1966. *Pekka und sein Pony*. Maier, 1967.

GRÜGER, Johannes. Born 1906 in Breslau, lives in Germany. During his studies in the theatre classes of the Breslau school of industrial design he brought into being an idea of his brother's, a musician, whereby the notes in children's songs were given the form of tiny, drawn objects. These *Liederfibel* (*Singing primers*) appeared in three volumes at Breslau 1927–33. After the Second World War he made a fresh start, working in many fields; advertising, book-jacket design, stained-glass windows, murals. His many picture-books often use bright colours in their treatment of popular subjects. (p. 104)

Grüger, H. *Liederfibel*. Brentano, 1949. Steuben, F. *Und Gott schuf Himmel und Erde*. Herder, 1958. Busta. C. *Die Sternenmühle*. Müller, 1959. Kopisch, A. *Die Heinzelmännchen*. Peters, n.d. Hoffmann, H. *Bilder für Kinder aus dem Leben Jesu*. Patmos, 1966; translated as *Children's Life of Jesus*. Helicon, 1966.

HAACKEN, Frans. Born 1911 in Aachen, lives in Holstein (East Germany); active as an advertising artist after studying at the Aachen school of industrial design. He has designed posters and cartoon films and illustrated periodicals and books, including work by Brecht and stories by Lisa Tetzner. He has created very few picture-books. (p. 92)

Das Loch in der Hose. Kinderbuchverlag, 1951. Prokofiev, S. *Peter und der Wolf*. Holz; Parabel, 1958. Translated as *Peter and the Wolf*. Bancroft, 1961; Watts, 1962.

HADER, Berta and Elmer Stanley. Berta born 'at a date which she does not like to think of' in Mexico, Elmer 1889 in California; they live in New York State. Elmer had experience of several jobs before entering art school at the age of seventeen. Through scholarships and by working as an actor he earned enough for a period of study in Paris and England. In 1914 he returned to America and after war service he married Berta Hoerner (1919). She had begun to write and draw very early on and after their marriage the couple began to publish books for children, working out their ideas for stories and pictures together. They share a sense of community with nature which is heightened by their 'lifetime task' of building and working on their woodland house. They were awarded the 1949 Caldecott Medal for *The big snow*. (p 193)

Chicken little; Hansel and Gretel; Ugly duckling; Wee Willie Winkie. Macmillan, N.Y., 1927. *The picture-book of travel.* Macmillan. N.Y. 1928. Meigs, C. *Lions, tigers and elephants too.* Longmans, N.Y., 1930. *Billy Butter.* Macmillan, N.Y., 1936. *Stop, look, listen.* Longmans, N.Y., 1936. *Cock a doodle do.* Macmillan, N.Y., 1939. *Pancho.* Macmillan, N.Y., 1942; R. Hale, 1946. *A picture book of Mother Goose.* Macmillan, N.Y., 1944. *The little stone house.* Macmillan, N.Y., 1944. *The mighty hunter*, Macmillan, N.Y., 1947; R. Hale, 1948. *The big city.* Macmillan, N.Y., 1947. *The big snow.* Macmillan, N.Y., 1948. *Ding dong bell.* Macmillan, N.Y., 1957.
BIB. Mahony, 413; Viguers, 227.
BIOG. Mahony, 314; Caldecott (1) by Rose Dobbs; HB (August 1928) by L. Seaman; Kunitz 148-50; Hader B. and E. *Working together.* Macmillan, N.Y., 1937.

HALE, Kathleen. Born 1898 in Scotland, lives in Hertfordshire. While still at school she showed a gift for drawing and later gained scholarships for study. She pushed forward with her work as a design artist while working at several other jobs, but after her marriage she began to produce the *Orlando* books for her own children (p. 110), finding few suitable picture-books available apart from the *Babar* books. *Orlando keeps a dog* is illustrated with pictures of her own house and its surroundings.

Orlando, the marmalade cat. Country Life, 1938. *Orlando, a camping holiday.* Country Life, 1938; Transatlantic, 1960. *Orlando's evening out.* Penguin, 1941; Transatlantic, 1962. *Orlando keeps a dog.* Country Life, 1948. *Henrietta, the faithful hen.* 2nd ed. Murray, 1950; Allen & Unwin, 1967. *Orlando and the three graces.* Murray, 1965 (and other Orlando titles).
BIOG. Viguers, 124-5; Hale, K., *All about Orlando.* Parents Review, and *Orlando's ballet* in HB (June 1953).

HALLER, Ruprecht. Lives in Solingen; served an apprenticeship in advertising in Leipzig. He worked as a book artist in Berlin-Pankow and is now a commercial and advertising artist in Solingen. His illustrations for picture-books have employed various techniques in accordance with the subject of the book. (p. 75)

Windmüller, J. Wir fahren aufs Land. Kinderbuchverlag, 1951. Schwarz, E. *Wiesenmusikanten.* Altberliner Verlag L. Groszer, 1953. Anand, M. *Mora.* Holz, 1960.

HENSCHEN, Helga. Born 1917 in Stockholm, lives in Sweden; brought up in a family of artists and thus appropriately trained. In addition to her work as a painter and sculptress she draws for magazines and illustrates children's books. (p. 97)

HERGÉ (i.e. Georges Rémi). After the First World War American comics began to arrive in Europe. M. Rémi, the employee of a Belgian newspaper, was given the job of creating something similar for the children's book supplement—and in this way Tintin the reporter arrived with Snowy at his heels. *Tintin au pays des Sovjets* was published in 1929 with many additional characters and under the pseudonym of Hergé. For every new volume in the series the artist and many reference assistants work together for nearly two years checking the authenticity of all the things and events which Hergé has drawn in what usually works out to be some 640 single pictures. (p. 175)

Tintin au pays des Sovjets. Casterman, 1929. Barret, A. *Tintin and the golden fleece.* A Tintin film book. Methuen, 1965. *The black island.* Methuen, 1966. (And many other titles.)

HERRMANN, Reinhard. Born 1923 in Münster where he now lives; studied art history at the University of Münster while at the same time attending the classes in graphic art at the college of technical art. After the war he turned his attention entirely to graphic art and in 1960 he became the director of courses in graphic art at Münster. His enthusiasm for the main subject of his work—illustrations for Bible stories—was aroused in childhood, for his father, a theologian, was a collector of early Bible illustrations. (pp. 156-7)

Die Arche Noah. Gütersloh, 1959. Translated as *Noah's ark.* Macmillan, 1962. Kuhne, H. *Die Schöpfung.* Gütersloh, 1961. Translated as *The creation.* Macmillan, 1962. (And further Bible stories also published by Macmillan.)

HEUCK, Sigrid. Born 1932 in Cologne, lives in the countryside near Munich; attended the Munich College of Art. Her mother's pony farm provides her with ideas and enthusiasm for her picture-books. She shows animals whose wishes are fulfilled through fairy-tale happenings and has a variety of graphic techniques at her command from montage work to linocuts. (p. 115)

Das Mondkuhparadies. Atlantis, 1959. Ruck-Pauquet, G. *Pony.* Atlantis, 1961. *Der Vogelbaum.* Betz, 1963. Neumann, R. *Das ganz besondere Tier.* Obpacher, n.d. Brandts, L. *Die Henne Gudula.* Betz, 1965.

HILL, Oliver. Born 1887 in London; has worked as a draughtsman and architect. (p. 184). *See also* under Tisdall, H.

HIM, George: *see* under Lewitt, Jan.

HLAVATÝ, Vladimír. Born 1934, lives in Czechoslovakia. He has illustrated children's verses by the German poet Morgenstern, together with children's books by Czech authors. (p. 119)

HOFFMANN, Felix. Born 1911 in Aarau, where he now lives. His childhood was influenced by the literary and musical interests of his parents and he received his training at various schools of art. In 1935 he returned to Aarau as a drawing tutor, but soon had to reduce his timetable in order to be able to work at glass-painting, murals, graffiti, and water-colours. His etchings, woodcuts, and lithographs ornament many books both for children and adults—some of them for the collector's market, however. His illustrations for fairy tales were designed for his own children, who also acted as models for some of the characters portrayed. These picture-books, together with a picture Bible, have appeared in various foreign editions. In 1957 he was awarded the *Schweizerische Jugendbuchpreis* 'for his superb work in the field of children's book illustration'. (pp. 16, 158)

Rapunzel. Amerbach, 1949; reissued by Sauerländer, 1960. *Der Wolf und die sieben Geisslein.* Sauerländer, 1957. *Dornröschen.* Sauerländer, 1959. *Die sieben Raben.* Sauerländer, 1962. *Joggeli wott go Birli schüttle.* Sauerländer, 1963. *Die vier kunstreichen Brüder.* Sauerländer, 1966. Translated as *Rapunzel* (1960), *The wolf and the seven little kids* (1958), *The sleeping beauty* (1959), *The seven ravens* (1963), *A boy went out to gather pears* (1966) and *The four clever brothers* (1967); all O.U.P. and Harcourt. Haviland, V. *Favourite fairy tales told in Poland.* Little, 1963; Bodley, 1966.
BIOG. Viguers, 128. Tschopp, C. *Felix Hoffmann als Illustrator.* Tschudy, 1957.

HONEGGER-LAVATER, Warja. Born 1913 in Winterthur, lives in Paris; spent much of her youth in Russia, Greece, and Switzerland

and trained as a graphic artist in schools at Zürich, Sweden, and Paris. She worked with and married Gottfried Honegger, and has been active in several fields. She designed and later edited the periodical *Jugend-Woche*; she has gained experience in many graphic techniques, has undertaken murals and illustrated children's books. In a series of folding books she has attempted to tell traditional stories by means of an abstract sign-language. (p. 177)

Sandy und die Kinder. Juwo, 1950. *Tyl Ulenspiegel*. Barfüsser, 1951. *Die Geschichte von Wilhelm Tell*. Basilius, 1962; translated as *William Tell*. Museum of Modern Art, 1962. *Hans im Glück*. Basilius, 1965. *Das hässliche junge Entlein*. Basilius, 1965. *Lechaperon rouge*. Maeght, 1967.

HORIUCHI, Seiichi. Born 1932 in Tokyo, lives in Japan. His readings of the classic books of Japan in adolescence made more impression on him than the Second World War and its consequences. He has studied political economy, and in 1961 he visited Europe. His attraction to books and the influence of his father, who is a painter, have determined his career as an illustrator. (p. 159)

HOWARD, Alan. Born 1922 in England. At the age of thirty, having read classics and history at Cambridge, he turned to art and is especially attracted by Henri Rousseau, Brueghel, and Botticelli. His illustrations for picture-books show a particular gift for representing animals and plants, perhaps best seen in *Peter and the wolf*. (pp. 33 and 78)

Prokofiev, S. *Peter and the wolf*. Faber, 1951; Barnes, 1953. Hutchinson, E. *Roof-top world*. Faber, 1956. Walker, D. E. *Fat cat Pimpernel*. Faber, 1958; Barnes, 1959. Lines, K. (ed.) *The Faber storybook*. Faber, 1961. Coe, R. *Crocodile*. Faber, 1964; Transatlantic, 1966. Tomlinson, J. *The bus that went to church*. Faber, 1966. Lines, K. (ed.). *Tales of magic and enchantment*. Faber, 1966. Tomlinson, J. *Patti finds an orchestra*. Faber, 1966. Browning, R. *The pied piper of Hamelin*. Faber, 1967. *Dick Whittington and his cat*. Faber, 1967.

JACOUTON, Jean. Born 1933 in St. Vallier, Drôme, lives in Paris. Work in advertising and fashion and as a shop-window and exhibition designer and as a teacher of drawing has alternated with studies and diploma examinations at art schools. His first pictures for religious children's books were made in 1963. (p. 155)

Elie et le feu du ciel. Cerf, *Le jeune David*. Cerf, 1963. Translated in the Dove Books Series. G. Chapman, 1965.

JANEČEK, Ota. Born 1919 in Pardubicky, lives in Prague. Having devoted the years 1938–41 to studying art he worked as a sculptor and designed patterns for textiles and wallpapers. In 1958 he was artistic director of a film which gained honours at Venice. He is also a member of the editorial staff of a journal of graphic art. He has carried out tours of study and has exhibited both at home and abroad. (colour illus., p. 7)

Halas, F. *Kinderparadies*. Dausien, 1960. Wallo, K. *Die Prinzessin mit dem goldenen Stern*. Artia, 1960. Macleod, A. *English fairy tales*. Hamlyn, 1966.

JANOSCH (i.e. Horst Eckert). Born 1931 in Zaborze on the German–Polish border, lives in Germany. He worked for two years in a Polish smithy and came to Germany at the age of fifteen. For four years he did unskilled work in a textile factory and was a pupil of the former Bauhaus professor Georg Muche. Later he studied at the Munich Academy. His first picture-book (1960) had its origin in the experiences of his childhood and in memories of tales told

him by his grandfather. It was the first of a series of books which he has written and illustrated himself. (p. 92)

Die Geschichte von Valek dem Pferd. Lentz, 1960. *Valek und Jarosch*. Lentz, 1960. Goethe, J. W. von. *Reineke Fuchs*. Lentz, 1962. *Das Auto hier heisst Ferdinand*. Parabel, 1964. *Das Apfelmännchen*. Parabel, 1965. Translated as *Just one apple*. Dobson; Walck, 1966. *Tonight at Nine*. Walck, 1967. *Der Josa mit der Zauberfiedel*. Parabel, 1967; translated as *Joshua and the magic fiddle*. World, 1968.

JANSSON, Tove. Born 1914 in Helsinki, lives in Finland, but writes in Swedish. She studied art and travelled abroad extensively. She paints landscapes and frescoes and designs stage sets. Although her first book was published in 1945, it was with the arrival of *Finn family Moomintroll* (Stockholm, 1949; London, Benn, 1950; Walck, 1965) that her fame began. In 1966 she added the Hans Andersen Medal to the various Scandinavian prizes which she had won. Of all the adventures which take place in Moominland, however, only two have been recorded in picture-book form. (p. 168)

The book about Moomin, Mymble and Little My. Benn, 1953. *Who will comfort Toffle?* Benn, 1960. *Exploits of Moomin pappa*. Walck, 1966. And others from Walck.
BIOG. Larsson, *Children's books in Sweden*. Stockholm, Swedish Institute for Children's Books, 1966.
CRIT. JB (December, 1966) by M. Crouch.

JARUSKA, Wilhelm. Born 1916 in Vienna, where he attended the school of industrial design and the academy of fine art. Besides illustrating children's books he has designed mosaics and murals and has worked as a painter and graphic artist. Since 1956 he has been professor in the technical design section of the Higher Graphic Teaching and Research Centre in Vienna. (p. 68)

Steiner, A. *Krikri das tapfere Entlein*. Jugend u. Volk, 1956. Translated as *Kriki the wild duck*. Harrap, 1959. Steiner, A. *Krikri und ihre Kinder*. Jugend u. Volk, 1959. Translated as *Kriki and the fox*. Harrap, 1960. Steiner, A. *Alle meine Pferde*. Jugend u. Volk, 1963. Translated as *All my horses*. Lerner, 1965.

JIMÉNEZ ARNALOT, M. Lives in Spain and illustrates popular books for small children. His picture-book, *Yo soy el gato*, was awarded the Lazarillo prize in 1960. (p. 76)

JONES, Harold. Born 1904 in London where he now lives. After a false start in the direction of farming, he turned to art and studied at evening classes before gaining a Royal Exhibition to the Royal College of Art. On leaving he became a teacher, but later turned to professional work. His picture-books (some of which were produced for his two daughters) have their origin in a water-colour technique which is completely and appealingly traditional, but which has an immediately recognizable individual style.

de la Mare, W. *This year next year*. Faber; Holt, 1937. *The visit to the farm*. Faber, 1941. *The enchanted night*. Faber, 1947. Lines, K. (comp.). *Lavender's blue*. O.U.P.; Watts, 1954. Lines, K. (comp.). *Once in Royal David's city*. O.U.P.; Watts, 1956. Blake, W. *Songs of innocence*. Faber; Barnes, 1961. Lines, K. (comp.). *Jack and the beanstalk*. O.U.P.; Watts, 1960. Lines, K. (comp.). *Noah and the ark*. O.U.P.; Watts, 1961. *Songs from Shakespeare*. Faber; Barnes, 1961. Browning, R. *The pied piper of Hamelin*. O.U.P.; Watts, 1962.
BIOG. Viguers, 136–7; JB (December 1948) by G. Collins.

KARÁSEK, Arnošt. Born 1919. The illustrations in his books for children reflect the mysterious, fairy-tale atmosphere of his chosen texts most impressively. (colour illus., p. 51)

KASSER, Helen. Born 1913, lives in Herrliberg, Switzerland; spent four years at the Zürich school of industrial design, where she studied under Ernst Gubler, Otto Meyer-Amden, Otto Morach, and Walter Roshardt. After working primarily in the field of advertising she turned to painting. The animals take pride of place in her picture-books, either freely presented on their own or worked into versions of fairy tales. (p. 69)

Andersen, H. C. *Das hässliche Entlein*, 1959. Kipling, R. *Die Katze, die für sich allein ging*, 1961. *Tiere in Feld und Wald*, 1962. (All Artemis.)

KEATS, Ezra Jack. Born 1916 in Brooklyn, where he now lives. He has been drawing and painting since childhood and was a graphic artist and muralist before beginning to illustrate children's books. He has also contributed designs to the UNICEF series of holiday cards. In 1963 he was awarded the Caldecott Medal for *The snowy day*.

Carpenter, F. *Wonder tales of cats and dogs*. Doubleday, 1955. Albee, G. S. *Three young kings*. Watts, 1956. *The snowy day*. Viking, 1962; Bodley, 1967. Tooze, R. *Our rice village in Cambodia*. Viking, 1963. *Whistle for Willie* Viking, 1964; Bodley, 1966. McGovern, A. *Zoo, where are you?* Harper, 1964. *John Henry*. Pantheon, 1965. Keats, John. *The naughty boy*. Viking, 1965; Whiting, 1966. *God is in the mountains*. Holt, 1966. *Jennie's hat*. Harper, 1966.
BIOG. Viguers, 139; Fuller, 120; Caldecott (2) by Esther Hautzig.
BIB. Viguers, 231.

KEEPING, Charles. Born 1924 in Lambeth and apprenticed in the printing trade at fourteen; he also worked as an engineer before serving in the Royal Navy. On leaving the Navy he studied graphic processes at the Regent Street Polytechnic, where he is now a visiting teacher in lithography. Lithographs by him have been exhibited at and purchased by museums and galleries in Great Britain and the United States. Some of his early work in picture-books was done for factual books but he has recently produced several original picture stories in which he has made imaginative use of memories of his own urban childhood.

Hogben, L. *Man must measure*. Rathbone; (U.S.A. title *The wonderful world of mathematics*. Doubleday, 1955). Murphy, J. S. *Bridges*. O.U.P., 1958. Foote, G. *Merrily on high*. O.U.P., 1959. *Shaun and the cart-horse*. O.U.P., Watts, 1966. *Black Dolly*. Brockhampton, 1966; U.S. title, *Molly o' the moors*. World, 1966. *Charley, Charlotte and the golden canary*. O.U.P.; Watts, 1967. *Tinker Tailor*. Brockhampton, 1968.

KILIAN, Adam. Born 1923 in Lemberg, lives in Warsaw. His mother was a professional art-critic and herself undertook his early training in art. During the war he studied architecture and art-history in England, returning to further studies in Poland in 1948. He became a stage-designer and director and was associated with the production of puppet films and film cartoons. He is a regular contributor to the magazine *Poland* and has illustrated many Polish picture-books. (p. 105)

Topelius, Z. *Die grosse Reise des kleinen Lutz*. Holz, 1964.

KLEMKE, Werner. Born 1917 in Berlin, lives in East Berlin where he is a professor; largely self-taught. He began by designing cartoon films and after the war was active as an advertising artist. Now his main activity is in 'making books', by which he means the selection and organization of text, paper and typography. He has every graphic technique at his command but allows his work to be influenced by the opinions of his children. (p. 87)

Michalkow, S. *Der Löwe und der Hase*. Holz, 1954. Rodrian, F. *Das Wolkenschaf*. Kinderbuchverlag, 1958. Rodrian, F. *Hirsch Heinrich*. Kinderbuch-

verlag, 1960. Translated as *Hubert the deer*. Benn, 1963. Rodrian, F. *Die Rakete von Bummelsburg*. Kinderbuchverlag, 1963. Fühmann, F. *Reineke Fuchs*. Kinderbuchverlag, 1964. Leaf, M. *The story of Ferdinand*. Viking, 1936; translated as *Ferdinand der stier*. Parabel, 1966.
BIOG. Ryder, 94–95; Nowak, B. *Werner Klemke*. Dresden, 1963.

KÜHN, Jörg. Born 1940, died 1964; studied commercial art and graphic processes at Zürich. He turned his attention entirely to scientific drawing and worked for the Zoological Institute of Zürich University. Fundamental studies in natural history were the basis of his only children's book on woodland animals. (p. 43)

Ziswiler, V. *Der Wald und seine Tiere*. Atlantis, 1963.

KUSKIN, Karla. Born in New York, lives in America. While still at school she was writing and illustrating picture-books and at the Yale School of Drawing she prepared a thesis on children's books. The book which she included in it as an example (*Roar and more*) was published by Harper's in 1956. It has been followed by further picture-books, all characterized by a strong sense of humour. (pp. 114 and 153)

Roar and more. Harper, 1956. *James and the rain*. Harper, 1957; Lutterworth, 1960. *The animals and the ark*. Harper, 1958; Lutterworth, 1961. Seidman, M. S. *Who woke the sun?* Macmillan, N.Y., 1960. *All sizes of noises*. Harper, 1962. *The rose on my cake*. Harper, 1964.

LADA, Josef. Born 1887 in Hrusice, Czechoslovakia, died 1957. As a cobbler's lad he grew up in primitive circumstances, but fought a way through for himself to the Prague school of industrial art. Apprenticed in bookbinding and barely fifteen years old he offered some sketches to the editors of the periodical *Maj* and some of these were actually printed. Later he worked as a draughtsman and cartoonist for newspapers, painted stage-sets, and illustrated books. He became known in Western Europe for his illustrations to *The good soldier Schweik;* children have loved him for his book about a talking cat whose text he wrote himself and whose pictures have a rich simplicity. (p. 93)

Purrkin the talking cat. Hasek, Jaroslav. *The good soldier Schweik*. Ungar, 1962. Harrap, 1966.
BIOG. Novotny, J. A. *Ladova ilustrace*. Prague, 1957 (includes a bibliography). Lada, J. *Ein Schusterbub wird Maler*. Berlin, Kinderbuchverlag. Ladova, A. *Muj táta Josef Lada*. Prague, Mladá fronta, 1963.

LANDEN, Elisabeth. Born 1930 in South Germany, lives in Sweden; 1948–54 studied painting in Karlsruhe, Munich, and Paris. In 1955 she married and went to live in Sweden. She does graphic work for daily newspapers and illustrates text books, reading books, and other children's books, among them a series of Bible stories for very young children. (p. 152)

LEBEDEV, Vladimír Vasilievich. Born 1891 in Leningrad, lives in Russia. As a schoolboy he worked in an art studio before beginning his own course of studies at the academy of fine arts in Leningrad, where he was later to teach as professor. He was one of the founders of the Soviet school of political poster artists; at the same time he has illustrated many children's books by such famous Russian authors as Marschak and Tolstoy. (p. 127)

The three bears. Foreign Languages Publishing House, n.d.

LE FOLL, Alain F. Born 1934 in France, lives in Paris. Since 1957 he has worked as a graphic artist and illustrator for magazines and publicity departments of companies in various Western countries.

His first children's books, chiefly religious in content, appeared in 1963. (p. 152)

Jésus au bord du lac, 1963. *Noé*, 1964. *Elysée guérit Naaman*, 1965. (All Cerf.) Translated in the Dove Books Series. G. Chapman, 1965.

LEMKE, Horst. Born 1922 in Berlin, has been living in Tessin since 1960. He had to leave school six months before his final exams because of a 'drawing' of Goebbels which he had made. He later studied at the Berlin college of fine arts, but was called up in 1941. Since his return he has worked for a magazine; he has also worked in advertising and as a freelance painter, especially as an illustrator for various children's books. (p. 166)

Denneborg, H. M. *Kasperle* series. Maier, 1963–. Krüss, J. *Zehn kleine Negerlein*. Mohn, 1963. Morgenstern, C. *Kindergedichte*. Überreuter, 1965.

LENICA, Jan. Born 1928 in Poznan; studied music, then graduated as a civil engineer in architecture; published funny drawings in a satirical magazine whose staff he joined. He broadened his field of activity as an artist by working on experimental films, gaining various prizes, also by illustrating children's books and by occasional work as a journalist, art critic, and architect. (p. 187)

Tuwim, J. *Die Lokomotive*. Hoffmann, 1958.
CRIT. *Polish posters and children's books* in *Graphis* (no. 27, 1949) by the artist himself.

LE SCANFF, Jacques. Born 1932 in Paris where he now lives; after a brief period of studying art he turned his hand to various jobs. Since 1950 he has concerned himself chiefly with painting, but has also practised sculpture and photography; his latest interest is in films. His first picture-book appeared in 1963 and has been followed by several others, all on religious themes. (p. 154)

Jonas, 1963. *Le paralytique guéri*, 1964. *Le baptême de Jésus*, 1964. *Abraham*, 1965. (All Cerf.) Translated in the Dove Books Series. G. Chapman, 1965.

LEWITT, Jan and HIM, George. Born 1907 and 1900 respectively, both live in England. Lewitt spent his childhood in Poland and later travelled in Europe and the Middle East; he undertook a number of jobs through which he acquired an understanding of art. Back in Poland in 1933 he met his fellow countryman George Him who had studied religion and educated himself in graphic art at Leipzig. They worked together as advertising artists and illustrators and in 1938 moved their studio to London. This occurred soon after the appearance of their first book for children—illustrations to four poems by Juljan Tuwim, *Lokomotywa* (Warsaw, 1938). Their bold designs and exciting use of colour had a considerable influence on contemporary book illustration. In 1954 the partnership ended and Lewitt, as Jan le Witt, continued work as an illustrator and costume designer, and George Him continued in graphic art, returning as a children's book artist in 1964. (p. 186)

Tuwim, J. *Locomotive*. Minerva, 1939. *The football's revolt*. Country Life, 1939; Sylvan, 1944; Transatlantic, 1945. Ross, D. *The little red engine gets a name*. Faber, 1942; Transatlantic, 1945. *Blue Peter*. Faber, 1943; Transatlantic, 1945. *Five silly cats*. Minerva, 1944. Le Witt, J. (only). *The vegetabull*. Collins; Harcourt, 1956. Him, G. (only). *The giant Alexander* series by Frank Herrmann; Methuen, 1964–; McGraw-Hill, 1965. Potter, S. *Squawky*. Heinemann; Lippincott, 1964. Berg, L. *Folk Tales*. Brockhampton; World, 1966.

LINDBERG, Stig. Born 1916 at Umea, Sweden, lives at Gustavsberg in Sweden. Owing to an injured finger he was unable to complete his studies as a pianist so turned to painting and was attracted to work with modelling materials. He was trained at Paris and became artistic director of the Gustavsberg porcelain factory where he fostered the idea of Swedish ceramics. He has also taught and lectured. His creative energy has found expression in industrial arts and crafts, textile design, posters, murals, and witty illustrations for children's books. (colour illus., p. 38)

Hellsing, L. and Strøyer, P. *Billy Potter buys a lollipop*. McGraw, 1961. Issued in England as *Billy's birthday lollipop*. Burke, 1966.

LOBEL, Arnold. Born 1933 in Los Angeles, lives in Brooklyn; studied at the Pratt Institute, New York. He began by illustrating books for Jewish children, followed by work in the first-reader series *I-can-read*. His first real picture-book—*A zoo for Mr. Muster*—appeared in 1962, having been inspired by frequent visits to the zoo with his own two children (p. 137).

A zoo for Mr. Muster. Harper, 1962. Phleger, F. *Red Tag comes back*. Harper, 1961; World's Work, 1962 (and other *I-can-read* books). Baker, B. *Little Runner of the Long House*. Harper; World's Work, 1962. *Giant John*. Harper, 1964; World's Work, 1965. *Martha the movie mouse*. Harper, 1966; World's Work, 1967.

LÖFGREN, Ulf. Born 1931, lives in Sweden. His first picture-book illustrations were made for stories by Leif Krantz, and the two artists are equal in the richness of their imagination and in their sense of humour. They were awarded the Nils Holgersson Plaque for the book about children in the jungle (p. 140), but in addition to their work together, Löfgren has illustrated two books with texts by himself.

Lindgren, A. and Krantz, L. *Die Kinder im Dschungel*, 1960. Krantz, L. *Die Kinder in der Luft*, 1963. (Both Oetinger.)

LUZZATI, Emanuele. Born 1921 in Genoa, where he still lives today. During the war he was in Switzerland where he attended a school of industrial design, but in 1945 he returned to Italy. He has worked as a stage-designer, illustrator, and ceramic artist. In collaboration with other artists he has drawn three cartoon films from which, together with Giulio Gianini, he has created three picture-books of the same title. (Colour illus., p. 49)

I Paladini di Francia, 1962. Rodari, G. *Castello di carte*, 1963. *La gazza ladra*, 1964. (All Mursia.)

McKEE, David. Born 1935 in South Devon; attended art school. After completion of military service he worked in London chiefly as a caricaturist. He now lives in Devon with his wife and two children, draws cartoons for periodicals such as *Punch* and paints abstracts. (p. 118)

Bronto's wings. Dobson, 1964. *Two can toucan*. Abelard, 1965. Grimm J. and W. *Hans in luck*. Abelard, 1967.

MAILLARD, Katharina. Born 1922 in Berlin, lives in Stuttgart. As the daughter of a teacher at the Berlin College of Art Education and as the mother of two children her work as a picture-book artist is a natural extension of personal background. Much of the pleasure in her picture-books and school-books lies in her very individual technique. (p. 81)

Arche Noah. Stalling, 1956. Appeared in England as *Noah's ark*. Blond, 1960. Krüss, J. *Kinder, heut ist Wochenmarkt*, 1957. Hille-Brandts, L. *Ich bin das kleine Steffelchen*, 1960. Rebay, T. v. *Das Märchen vom Fischer und seiner Frau*, 1961. Hanisch, H. *Der kleine Herr Pucha und sein Hähnchen Koko*, 1963. Alverdes, P. *Vom Schlaraffenland*, 1965. (All Stalling.)

MAITLAND, Antony. Born 1935 in Andover, but spent his childhood in the Mendip country; he now lives in London. Having gained a diploma at the West of England College of Art, Bristol, in 1957, he spent two years in the army and then a year travelling with the aid of a Leverhulme Scholarship. On returning to England he was commissioned to illustrate *Mrs. Cockle's cat* with which he won the Kate Greenaway Medal for 1961. He now works as a freelance artist and has illustrated many children's novels as well as picture-books. (p. 173)

Pearce, P. *Mrs. Cockle's cat*. 1961; Lippincott, 1962. *The secret of the shed*. 1962; Meredith, 1963. Molloy, A. *A proper place for chip*. 1963; Hastings, 1963. *Ben goes to the city*, 1964. *James and the Roman silver*, 1965. (All first published in England by Constable.)

MAJO, Ennio di. Born 1931 in Tripoli, lives in Italy; self-taught. He works as a stage-designer and designer of puppet films for Italian television. Fantasy predominates in his illustrations for picture-books, several of which have been translated into other languages. (p. 91)

Anguissola, G. *L'inviata specialissima*. Mursia, 1959. Rascel, R. *Piccoletto*. Mursia, 1960. Translated under the same title, Pantheon, 1961. Krüss, J. *Michele-Guck-Dich-Um*. Obpacher, 1961. Rascel, R. *Renatino non vola la domenica*. Mursia, 1962.

MATHIESEN, Egon. Born 1907 in Esbjerg, Denmark, lives in Copenhagen. As a child he painted and drew a great deal, but since he had paper but no colours he utilized such things as toothpaste, brick dust, and his father's tailor's chalks. Although self-taught he has gained a government award for his picture-books, which are created from a knowledge of children's particular needs where art is concerned. (p. 63)

Blue-eyed Pussy. Doubleday, 1951. *Oswald the monkey*. Macdowell, 1959. *Jungle in the wheatfield*. Macdowell, 1960.
BIOG. Viguers, 155.
CRIT. *The artist and the picture book* in HB (February 1966) by the artist himself.

MAYO, Eileen. Born in Norwich, lives in New Zealand; studied painting and learned from Fernand Léger the art of the colour woodcut. Most of her work has appeared in periodicals; her picture-books are mostly associated with natural history. (p. 185)

Shells and how they live. Pleiades, 1944; Transatlantic, 1945. *Story o living things*. Gawthorn; Maclelland, 1944. *Little animals of the countryside*. Pleiades; Transatlantic, 1945. *Larger animals of the countryside*. Pleiades; Ambassador, 1949. *Animals on the farm*. Penguin, 1951.

MONTESANTOU, Louisa. Born 1917 in Athens where she now lives; studied art in Paris, Vienna, and Budapest. Exhibitions of her work have been held in Europe and elsewhere; she has illustrated some twenty picture-books. (p. 101)

MONTRESOR, Beni. Born 1926 in Verona, lives in America; received his training in art at Verona, Venice, and Rome. He has designed stage sets and costumes for film, theatrical and operatic productions in several European countries and his *Cinderella* is based upon stage designs for a production of Rossini's opera at the

Metropolitan. At the age of twenty he wrote five radio plays for young listeners and has since written children's fairy stories, all of which have had a wide audience. He was awarded the Caldecott Medal in 1965 for *May I bring a friend?* (p. 120)

Brown, M. W. *On Christmas eve*. Scott, 1961. Johnson, S. P. *The princesses*. Harper, 1962. *House of flowers, house of stars*. Knopf, 1962. de Regniers, B. S. *May I bring a friend?* Atheneum, 1964; Collins, 1966. *Cinderella*. Knopf, 1965; Collins, 1967. *I saw a ship a sailing*. Knopf, 1967.
BIOG. Caldecott (2) by V. V. Varner.

MOREU, René. Born 1920 at Nizza, lives in France; he worked at a printer's and trained himself as a painter at schools of art. He is friendly with André François, has worked in several children's periodicals and had illustrated over twenty books since 1953. (p. 195)

Ollivier, J. *Aux quatre coins du pré*, 1958. Ollivier, J. *Chacun fait son nid*, 1960. Ollivier, J. *Les saltimbanques*, 1962. Gamarra, P. *Chansons de ma façon*, 1963. (All Farandole.) Schnitzer, L. *La montagne du souriceau*. Flammarion, 1963. Raymond, J. *Hélène et les oiseaux*. Farandole, 1965.

MOSER, Rudolf. Born 1914, lives in Berne; a course in advertising art at the Zürich School of Industrial Design was followed by a period of study under famous teachers at Munich. From 1939 to 1942 he was a designer of film cartoons at Berne. He illustrated newspapers and school-books as well as children's books, but his only picture-book so far has been inspired by the flight of a fairground balloon, and is partly based on his own experience. (p. 169)

Zötti und Balloni. Atlantis, 1959.

MUNARI, Bruno. Born 1907 in Milan, where he now lives. He began his career as a futurist painter and achieved fame as a maker of mobiles and toys. As a book-designer he began to produce children's books in 1945, creating volumes with all sorts of amusing surprises in them—pictures with flaps in them which revealed other pictures underneath, or pages which altered size according to the progress of the story. (p. 61). Out of print in Italy, these have been re-issued in the United States together with an ABC, a zoo book, and several books stemming from basic ideas about design.

Gigi cerca il suo berretto. Mondadori, 1945. Translated as *Georgie has lost his cap*. Harvill, 1953 and *Jimmy has lost his cap*. World, 1959. *L'uomo del camion*. Mondadori, 1945. Translated as *Lorry driver*. Harvill, 1953, and *The birthday present*. World, 1959. *Mai contenti*. Mondadori, 1945. Translated as *What I'd like to be*. Harvill, 1953, and *The elephant's wish*. World, 1959. *Storia di tre uccellini*. Mondadori, 1945. Translated as *Tic tac and toc*. World, 1957. *Il venditore di animali*. Mondadori, 1945. Translated as *Animals for sale*. World, 1957. *Toc, toc, chi è? apri la porta*. Mondadori, 1945. Translated as *Who's there?* World, 1957. *ABC*. World, 1960. *Zoo*. World, 1963.
BIOG. Veronesi, G. *Munari in Graphis* (no. 61, 1955)

MUNOA, Rafael. Born 1930 in San Sebastian where he now lives. A sensitive and often humorous draughtsman, his work for young people (illustrations to factual books, to retellings of legends and to literary texts) has several times gained awards of merit. (p. 36)

MURATA, Michinori. Born 1924 in Aichi Province, Japan. After concluding his studies in drawing he illustrated a children's encyclopaedia and a book about building a new house. With this work as a basis and with a strong inclination to continue drawing for children, he would like his future picture-books to deal with factual subjects. (p. 182)

NAKATANI, Chiyoko. Born 1930 in Tokyo where she now lives; 1952, concluded her art studies at Tokyo University. She married a painter and was for a time a teacher of drawing. In 1963 she had a long period of study in Europe. Paintings for her picture-books are done in oils and she hopes through them to awaken an understanding of good art in young children. The texts for these books have all been written by the poetess Eriko Kishida. (pp. 62–63)

Kishida, E. *Hippopotamus.* Prentice-Hall, 1963. *Wake up, hippopotamus.* Bodley, 1967. *The hippo boat.* Bodley, 1967; World, 1968. Alberti, T. *The Animals' lullaby.* Atlantis; Bodley; World; Fukuinkan-Shoten, 1967. Daudet, A. *The brave little goat of Monsieur Séguin.* Kaishei-sha, 1966; World, 1968. *The Day Chiro was Lost.* Fukuinkan-Shoten, 1965; Bodley, 1968; World, 1969.

NUSSBAUMER, Paul. Born 1934 at Lucerne in whose vicinity he still lives. After a five-year course of art study he spent six months in Rome and since then has worked as an advertising artist and designer of window displays; for the last four years he has worked freelance. He has a preference for landscape painting, but also draws abstracts. Since his marriage he has become interested in children's books and with his wife's encouragement he painted a number of picture-books, the first being published in 1964. (colour illus., p. 47)

Nussbaumer, M. *Ihr Kinderlein kommet.* Atlantis, 1964. Translated as *Away in a manger.* Constable; Harcourt, 1965. Hürlimann, B. *Der Knabe des Tell.* Atlantis, 1965. Translated as *William Tell and his son.* Harcourt, 1967. Hürlimann, B. *Barry.* Atlantis, 1967; Harcourt, 1968.

OBERLÄNDER, Gerhard. Born 1907 in Berlin, lives in Frankfurt; art training in Berlin. After the last war he worked as a church decorator in Würzburg, moving to Frankfurt in 1952. On the lookout for something new he here received a commission for a children's book and this, with others written by himself, was followed by illustrations for many classics both of children's and adult literature. Basing his work on pen-and-ink drawing he has developed a very individual style which is apparent even in work he may do in advertising or for the press. (p. 89)

Pienchen mit hartem P, 1954. *Krählinde die Aufgeplusterte,* 1956. *Das Märchen von den drei Apfelbäumen,* 1958. Baldner, G. *Joba und das Wildschwein,* 1961. A bi-lingual edition issued as *Joba and the wild boar.* Constable; Hastings, 1961. *Die Schnake Schnak,* 1963. La Fontaine. *Zwölf Fabeln,* 1965. Kopisch, A. *Die Heinzelmännchen,* 1967. (All Ellermann.)
BIOG. Halbey, H. A. *Gerhard Oberländer.* Offenbach, 1963.

OLSEN, I. S. Born 1921 in Copenhagen; studied at two different art schools, after which he was active chiefly as a designer, poster artist, and illustrator of books both for adults and children. His picture-books for children bear witness in words and pictures to his imagination and his wealth of comic ideas. (colour illus., p. 25)

The marsh crone's brew, 1960; *Lars-Peter's birthday; The boy in the moon.* (All Abingdon, 1963.)

OSTERC, Lidija. Born 1929 in Ljubljana, lives in Yugoslavia. Among other things she has illustrated a story from Grimm and a book on the Slovene language. (p. 163)

Peroci, E. *Das Haus aus Klötzchen.* Betz, 1965.

PAPAS, William. Born 1927 in South Africa; came to England at the end of the war and studied at Beckenham Art School. After two years travelling on the Continent, during which he forsook painting for sketching, he returned to South Africa as a cartoonist for the

Cape Times. This he abandoned in favour of farming and trading timber, but returned to England in 1959 as cartoonist for *The Guardian.* His love of cartoon techniques is clearly apparent in his picture-books, both in their witty drawing and in the sparing but highly expressive use of line and colour. (p. 30)

The Press. O.U.P., 1964. Downing, C. *Tales of the Hodja.* O.U.P., 1964; Walck, 1965. Stone, J. *The law.* O.U.P., 1966. *The story of Mr. Neró.* O.U.P.; Coward McCann, 1965. *Tasso.* O.U.P.; Coward McCann, 1966. Shrapnel, N. *Parliament.* O.U.P., 1966. Walsh, P. *Freddy the fell engine.* O.U.P., 1966. Moorhouse, G. *The Church.* O.U.P., 1967. *No Mules.* O.U.P.; Coward McCann, 1967. *Taresh the tea planter.* O.U.P., 1968.

PARAĆ, Dalibor. A Yugoslavian illustrator, professor at Zagreb. He has illustrated famous books for young people, such as *Robinson Crusoe,* has collaborated in a junior encyclopaedia and also illustrated school-books and collectors' editions. (p. 143).

PIATTI, Celestino. Born 1922 in Wangen, Switzerland, lives in Riehen; attended a school of commercial art and received training in graphic processes. 1948–49 he opened his own graphic studio with his wife as sole partner. The work he has done here—posters, prospectuses, the publicity for the German paperback publishers 'dtv'—displays the same features: great intensity achieved by the use of thick black outlines and strong colouring. In his illustrations to class-readers for Basel and in his picture-books, he is anxious for children to see well-designed, memorable images. (p. 67)

Eulenglück. Artemis, 1965. Translated as *The happy owls.* Benn; Atheneum, 1965. Schumacher, H. *ABC der Tiere.* Artemis, 1965. Translated as *An animal ABC.* Benn, 1965; Atheneum, 1966. Huber, U. *Zirkus Nock.* Artemis, 1967. Translated as *The Nock family circus.* Benn, 1967.

PLAUEN, E. O. (i.e. Erich Ohser). Born 1903 in Untergettengrün in Vogtland, died 1944; grew up in Plauen and studied at the Academy of Graphic Art, Leipzig. He illustrated books for his friend Erich Kästner; on moving to Berlin he put his opinions on national socialism into a series of caricatures, whereupon he was forbidden to draw. Under his pseudonym he worked at his 'Father and son' picture-stories (p. 174), which were printed between 1934 and 1937. He was later denounced as 'politically unreliable' and sentenced to death, but died by his own hand in prison.

Vater und Sohn. 3 vols. Ullstein, 1935–8 (Sudverlag, 1952). A selection published in the *Ravensburger Taschenbücher* (Maier).
BIOG. Kästner, E. *Heiteres von E. O. Plauen.* Hannover, 1957. Bohne, F. *E. O. Plauen.* Hannover, 1962.

PORTAL, Colette. A young French authoress who is married to the well-known graphic artist Michel Folon. Her first picture-book was originally published in Germany and depicts the life of the ants with a combination of poetry and factual detail. She is working on further books. (p. 86)

Das Leben einer Königin. Münchner Bilderbuchverlag, 1962. Translated as *The life of a queen.* Braziller, 1964; Cape, 1965.

PROVENSEN, Alice and Martin. Born 1918 and 1916 respectively in America; they both attended the School of the Chicago Art Institute, but only met and married after they had left. They now live on a farm in New York State. Most of their illustrative work is for texts of 'classic' status to which they bring a restraint and clarity of design which is as much decorative as it is illustrative. As such it is at its most successful in conjunction with the retellings of ancient myths and the New Testament Bible stories (p. 102).

Bom, M. B. *The fireside book of folk songs.* Simon, 1947. *The golden Mother Goose.* Simon, 1948; Purnell, n.d. Stevenson, R. L. *A child's garden of verses.* Simon, 1951; Hamlyn, n.d. *Animal fair.* Simon, 1952; Hamlyn, n.d. *The New Testament.* Simon, 1953; Purnell, n.d. Watson, J. W. *The Iliad and the Odyssey.* Golden Press, 1956; Hamlyn, n.d. White, A. T. *Myths and legends.* Golden Press, 1959; Hamlyn, n.d. Chaucer, G. *Canterbury tales.* Golden Press, 1961; Hamlyn, n.d. The *Karen* books. Golden Press, 1963; Collins, 1964. *Aesop's fables.* Golden Press; Hamlyn, 1965.
BIOG. Viguers, 168.

RAND, Paul. Born 1914 in Brooklyn, lives in Weston, Connecticut; studied at several schools of art; distinguished himself early on in the fields of advertising art, book design and fabric printing. At the age of twenty-three he was art director of the magazines *Esquire* and *Apparel arts*, but later moved on to university teaching. He has written a lot of articles and a book on design. His first picture-books broke new ground in their presentation of ideas and forms; they were produced for his own daughter and with the collaboration of his wife Ann, who studied architecture under Mies van der Rohe. (p. 179)

I know a lot of things, 1956. *Sparkle and spin,* 1957. *Little one,* 1962. (All Harcourt Brace and Collins.)
CRIT. Kamekura, Y. ed. *Paul Rand: his work from 1946 to 1958.* Knopf, 1959.

REIDEL, Marlene. Born 1923 at Landshut, Germany, lives in Germany; studied painting at Munich and married a sculptor. In order to show her four children how she had once lived on a farm she produced a picture-book for home consumption illustrated (appropriately) with potato cuts. To make her next book, *Kasimirs Weltreise,* available to more children she used linocuts for her pictures of foreign countries and strange customs. It is a technique which she has continued to employ in her subsequent picture-books. (colour illus., p. 10)

Kasimirs Weltreise, 1957. Translated as *Eric's journey.* Routledge, 1960. *Schlaf Kindlein schlaf,* 1959. *Die Hexenuhr,* 1960. (All Betz.) *Der Jakob und die Räuber,* 1965; translated as *Jacob and the Robbers.* Atheneum, 1967.

ROJANKOVSKY, Feodor Stepanovich. Born 1891 in Latvia, lives in Bronxville, New York. He was brought up in a highly gifted artistic family and was soon stirred by a love of nature and by looking at illustrated books in his father's library to draw for himself. At the age of eight he had made illustrations for *Robinson Crusoe*; at seventeen he completed a mural for a theatre in the Crimea and at twenty-one he entered the Moscow Fine Arts Academy. As a soldier during the war he drew for magazines and illustrated a picture-book; later, after various adventures, he arrived in Paris where he was 'discovered' by Esther Averill the American owner of the Domino Press. With her he published his first English picture-book, *Daniel Boone,* before placing his art at the service of Père Castor who had taken it upon himself to publish artistically satisfying picture-books at low prices. In 1941, with the coming of the German occupation, Rojankovsky sailed for America and has there given expression in many picture-books to his fondness for children, for nature and for art. He received the 1956 Caldecott Medal for *Frog went a-courtin'.* (p. 98)

Averill, E. *Daniel Boone.* Paris, Domino, 1931; 2nd edn, Harper, 1946. Lida. *Albums du Père Castor.* Paris, Flammarion, 1932–42. Translations published by Harper and Allen & Unwin. *Tall book of Mother Goose.* Harper, 1942; Ed. Ward, 1962. Kipling, R. Individual issues of tales from the *Just So Stories.* Garden City, 1942–47. Duplaix, G. *Animal stories.* Simon, 1944. *The Old Testament.* Simon, 1946; Purnell, n.d. Jackson, K. and B. *Big elephant.* Simon, 1949. *Great big animal book.* Simon, 1950. Koch, D. *I play at the beach.* Holiday, 1955. Langstaff, D. *Frog went a-courtin'.* Harcourt, 1955; World's Work, 1956. Thayer, J. *Outside cat.* Morrow, 1952; Brockhampton, 1958. *More Mother Goose.* Simon, 1958. Rand, A. *The little river.* Harcourt, 1959; World's Work, 1963. *Animals in the zoo.* Knopf, 1962. Rand, A. *So small.* Harcourt, 1963; World's Work, 1966. Memling, C. *I can count.* Golden, 1963. Memling, C. *Ten little animals.* Golden, 1965.
BIB. Mahony, 435; Viguers, 241.
BIOG. Mahony, 353–4; Viguers, 171–2; Caldecott (2) by E. Averill; HB (February 1932); Kunitz, 260–1.

ROSE, Gerald. Born 1935 in Hongkong, lives in England; the son of an English father and a Chinese mother he arrived in England in 1945 after four years of internment. He studied painting and now teaches at the Maidstone College of Art; he has also exhibited paintings. His picture-books are mostly tailored around stories by his wife Elisabeth and are notable for the delight of their colouring. He received the 1960 Kate Greenaway Medal for *Old Winkle and the seagulls.* (p. 72)

How St. Francis tamed the wolf. Faber, 1958; Harcourt, 1959. *Wuffles goes to town.* Faber, 1959; Barnes, 1960. *Old Winkle and the seagulls.* Faber, 1960; Barnes, 1961. *Charlie on the run.* Faber, 1961. Ireson, B. *The story of the pied piper.* Faber; Barnes, 1961. *The big river.* Faber, 1962; Norton, 1964; Hughes, P. *The emperor's oblong pancake.* Abelard, 1962. Pender, L. *Dan McDougall and the bulldozer.* Abelard, 1963. *Good king Wenceslas.* Faber, 1964; Transatlantic, 1965. *The magic suit.* Faber, 1966. (A retelling of 'The emperor's new clothes'.) *Tim's giant marrow.* Benn, 1966. *The sorcerer's apprentice.* Faber, 1966. Hughes, P. *Baron Brandy's boots.* Abelard, 1966. *Alexander's flycycle.* Faber, 1967. Jennings, P. *The great jelly of London.* Faber, 1967.

ROSER, Wiltrud. Born 1924 in Cham, Germany, where she now lives; she spent two years at the Free College of Art in Stuttgart. In 1953 she married, her husband being a marionette player who travels abroad extensively. She made her first picture-book for her son and in both its story and its illustrations it shows a sensitive feeling for the world of young children. The more demanding texts and illustrations of her later children's books reflect her son's own growing-up. (p. 83)

Die Pimpelmaus. Atlantis, 1958. *Schnick und Schnack.* Atlantis, 1959. *1000 Mark für Waldemar.* Buchheim, 1960. *Das Hündchen Benjamin.* Atlantis, 1962. *Die Vogelhochzeit.* Atlantis, 1964. *Wo sich Fuchs und Has gute Nacht sagen.* Atlantis, 1966.

ROTH-STREIFF, Lili. Born 1905 in Mollis, Switzerland, lives in Zürich; after attending the Basel school of design she studied under Fritz Ehmcke in the classes on graphic art at the Munich school of industrial design. She has illustrated texts both by herself and by other authors, together with a first reader for schools. These books have an appeal to readers who are looking for reflectiveness rather than mere graphic cleverness. (p. 82)

Paur-Ulrich, M. *Das Rösslein Kilian.* Atlantis, 1944. *Peters Weihnachtstraum.* Atlantis, 1946. *Der dumme August und die Tiere.* Büchergilde Gutenberg, 1953. *Mimosa.* Atlantis, 1961.

RUBIN, Eva Johanna. Born 1925, lives in Berlin; she is above all a draughtsman, a graphic artist. Her picture-books are published both in West and East Germany. The reason for the success of her coloured line-drawings lies in the powerful graphic effects which she is able to combine with exact objective representation. This points to a withdrawal from the artistic freedom of recent times. She was awarded a special picture-book prize for her illustrations to *3 × 3 an einem Tag* by James Krüss. (p. 106)

Krüss, J. *3 × 3 an einem Tag.* Betz, 1963. Translated as *3 × 3.* Methuen; Collier-Mac., 1965. Neumann, R. *Der böse Bär.* Betz, 1964. Translated as *The bad bear.* Methuen, 1967. *Himpelchen und Pimpelchen.* Kinderbuchverlag, 1964. Krüss, J. *Der Trommler und die Puppe.* Betz, 1966.

SÁNCHEZ PRIETO, Julio Antonio. Born 1926, lives in Madrid where he teaches drawing. He produces advertising and educational films, illustrates magazines, book-jackets, and, for his own preference, books for children and young people. His enthusiasm is particularly stirred by legends, sagas and classical tales from various countries. (p. 191)

Morales, R. *Das Vermächtnis des Sonnengottes.* Union, 1960.

SATO, Churyo. Born 1912 in the Miyagi province of Japan; concluded his study of sculpture at Tokyo. He has travelled in Siberia, China, and North Korea, and as a well-known realist sculptor he likes to work on representations of children. His fondness for children is also given expression in his picture-books, and he particularly likes illustrating Russian tales. (p. 162)

SCHEEL, Marianne. Born 1902 in Flensburg, lives in Munich; 1921–27 training at the Academy of Graphic Art and Book Design at Leipzig. She now works as a graphic artist and illustrator. The chief subject of her picture-books is nature in all its variety, but she has also been very active in the field of line illustration. In 1958 she received special acclaim for her book *Das Haus zum Regenbogen.* (pp. 5, 9, and 97)

Rinser, L. *Tiere in Haus und Hof.* Atlantis, 1943. Oswald, S. *Die Geschichte von der Wiese.* Atlantis, 1945. *Reise mit Zebi.* Stuffer, 1947. *Das Haus zum Regenbogen.* Atlantis, 1958. *Schornebogs Wald.* Atlantis, 1961. *Das bucklig Männlein und andere alte Kinderverse.* Atlantis, 1964. *Klein und gross.* Atlantis, 1965.

SCHWARZ, Liselotte. Born 1930 at Liegnitz, Silesia, lives in Hamburg. Today she is preoccupied chiefly with freelance graphic work, painting, and typography. Her pictures composed of torn pieces of coloured paper look as though they had been made by children, but they are very cunningly devised. She has made an essential contribution to raising the artistic quality of board-books for the youngest children. (p. 109)

Musch, die kleine Katze, 1957. *Leiermann dreht goldne Sterne,* 1959. *In einem kleinen Haus,* 1960. *Einen Löffel für den goldnen Hahn,* 1961. (All Ellermann.) The first, third, and fourth of these have been translated as *Mitzai, the little cat, In one little house,* and *A spoon for a golden rooster.* (All Follett, 1966.)

SENDAK, Maurice. Born 1928 in Brooklyn, New York, where he still lives. From the age of about four he was determined to be a writer and illustrator, and in fact illustrated his first book (*Atomics for the millions*) while still at school. After studying at the Art Students League he worked in window-display before being commissioned by Harper's to illustrate Marcel Aymé's *Wonderful Farm.* This led to his co-operation with Ruth Krauss on *A hole is to dig,*

after which he rapidly became established as one of the most versatile and sensitive illustrators working today. This was formally recognized by the award of the 1964 Caldecott Medal for *Where the wild things are.* (pp. 18, 84–85)

Aymé, M. *The wonderful farm.* Harper, 1951. Krauss, R. *A hole is to dig.* Harper, 1952; Hamilton, 1963. Krauss, R. *I'll be you.* Harper, 1954. Krauss, R. *Charlotte and the white horse.* Harper, 1955. Sendak, J. *The happy rain.* Harper, 1956; World's Work, 1959. *Very far away.* Harper, 1957; World's Work, 1960. Minarik, E. H. *Little bear,* 1957; World's Work, 1958. (And other books in this series.) Udry, J. M. *The moon jumpers.* Harper, 1959. *The nutshell library.* Harper, 1962; Collins, 1964. *Where the wild things are.* Harper, 1963; Bodley, 1967. Stockton, F. R. *The bee man of Orn* and *The griffin and the minor canon.* Holt, 1964; Collins, 1967. *Hector Protector.* Harper, 1965; Bodley, 1967.
BIB. JB (April 1966).
BIOG. Viguers, 176; Fuller, 181–2; Ryder, 114–15.
CRIT. HB (August 1956) by Barbara Cooney; JB (April 1966) by J. Dohm; CBN (March 1967) by B. W. Alderson.

SEWELL, Helen. Born 1896 in California, died 1957 in New York. As a small child she was taken to live on the Pacific island of Guam where she was profoundly impressed by the landscape. She wished very much to be an artist and on her father's death she returned to America and acquired for herself the necessary knowledge of techniques. Her activity as an illustrator stemmed from her close association with many young relatives and during her life she illustrated over sixty children's books, some of which she wrote herself. Among them is *Three tall tales,* an interesting attempt to use the techniques of the comic-strip in a creative way. (p. 150)

Rhys, M. *Mr. Hermit Crab.* Macmillan, N.Y., 1929. *ABC for everyday.* Macmillan, N.Y., 1930. *Blue barns.* Macmillan, N.Y., 1933; Woodfield, 1955. *A first Bible.* Oxford, 1934. Farjeon, E. *Ten Saints.* Oxford, 1936. *Peggy and Penny.* Oxford, 1937. Bulfinch, T. *A book of myths.* Macmillan, N.Y., 1942. *Three tall tales.* Macmillan, N.Y., 1947. *Birthdays for Robin.* Macmillan, N.Y., 1947; Hale, 1948. Grimm, J. and W. *Tales.* Oxford, N.Y., 1954. Evers A. *In the beginning.* Macmillan, N.Y., 1954. Evers, A. *Three kings of Saba.* Lippincott, 1955.
BIB. Mahony, 437; Viguers, 243.
BIOG. Viguers, 177; HB (March 1946; March 1948; October 1957); Kunitz, 271–2.

SHAAR, Pinchas. Born 1923 in Lodz, now divides his time between Israel and Paris. His training as an artist was interrupted by years spent in the ghetto, in a concentration camp and a refugee camp. In 1947 he came to Paris, where he studied painting, moving to Israel in 1951. Apart from illustrating children's books he also paints and has exhibited in Belgium, Paris, America, and Israel. (p. 107)

SIEMASŹKO, Olga (*née* Bielinska). Born 1914 in Kraków, lives in Warsaw; 1939 concluded her art studies and in 1945 she became editor of a children's magazine. Later she took up editorial duties in a large children's publishing house. Her love of children, her close sympathy for Polish tradition in children's books and her living sense of the world of fable combine to make her one of the best known of Polish picture-book illustrators. (p. 100)

CRIT. *Graphis* (no. 32, 1950) by Jan Lenica; *Thoughts on children's books in Poland* in *Graphis* (no. 131, 1967) by the artist herself.

SIMONT, Marc. Born 1915 in Paris, lives in New York and Cornwall, Connecticut. His parents were Spanish and his father was a well-known illustrator who was on the staff of the French art journal *L'illustration.* He attended various schools in France, Spain, and the U.S.A. before coming to Paris to study at two famous academies of art. He settled in America where he undertook military service and later married. As a children's book illustrator he is very critical in his selection of texts and has often resorted to supplying the stories for his pictures himself. He was awarded the 1957 Caldecott Medal for his illustrations to *A tree is nice*. (pp. 64 and 142)

De Jong, M. *Billy and the unhappy bull*. Harper, 1946. Lang, A. *The red fairy book*. Longmans, 1948. Krauss, R. *Happy day*. Harper, 1949. Krauss, R. *Backward day*. Harper, 1950. *Polly's oats*. Harper, 1951; Faber, 1953. *The lovely summer*. Harper, 1952; Faber, 1954. Fritz, J. *Fish head*. Coward, 1954; Faber, 1956. *Plumber out of the sea*. Harper, 1955. Udry, J. *A tree is nice*. Harper, 1956. Schwartz, J. *I know a magic house*. McGraw, 1956. *How come elephants?* Harper, 1965.
BIB. Viguers, 244.
BIOG. Viguers, 180; Caldecott (2) by E. Lansing; Fuller, 187–8.

SROKOWSKI, Jerzy. Born 1910 in Warsaw, lives in Poland; is now professor in the Academy of fine arts where he was once a student. Besides drawing and painting illustrations, posters, and cartoons he is also connected with the planning of Polish pavilions for fairs and exhibitions throughout the world. Along with other prizes he has gained an award for the illustration of children's books. (colour illus., p. 54)

STEFULA, Georgy. Born 1913 in Hamburg, of Hungarian parentage. He lives in Upper Bavaria with his wife Dorothea, who is also active as an artist. He works at painting, illustration, and advertising art and is self-taught. In the dictionaries he is described as a naïve painter and this naïvety is seen at its most expressive in the colour pictures for his children's book on the story of the Creation. (p. 151)

Das Paradies. Ellermann, 1955.

STOBBS, William. Born 1914 at South Shields, lives near Maidstone where he is Principal of the College of Art. After leaving Durham University with a degree in history he decided to study art and became very interested in all aspects of graphic work. Before going to Maidstone he was for eight years Head of the Design Department at the London School of Printing and it is therefore not surprising that his illustrations for both picture-books and children's novels are characterized by a strong feeling for page design. He was given the 1959 Kate Greenaway Award for his work in *Kashtanka* and *A bundle of ballads*. (p. 80)

Chekov, A. *Kashtanka*. O.U.P., 1959; Walck, 1961. Manning-Sanders, R. (compiler). *A Bundle of Ballads*. O.U.P., 1959; Lippincott, 1961. Cass, J. *The cat thief*. Abelard, 1961. (And other titles.) Hewett, A. *The little white hen*. Bodley, 1962. *The story of the three bears*. Bodley, 1964. *Jack and the beanstalk*. Constable, 1965. *The three little pigs*. Bodley, 1965. *The golden goose*. Bodley, 1966. *The three Billy Goats Gruff*. Bodley, 1967. Yolen, J. *Greyling*. World, 1968; Bodley, 1969.
CRIT. JB (July 1960) an autobiographical note. Ryder, 120–121.

STRØYER, Poul. Born 1923 in Copenhagen, lives in Stockholm, works chiefly as a cartoonist for big Swedish newspapers. Both the action and the pictures in his children's books are full of fantastic and comic situations, especially in those books where he has himself devised the story. In his illustrations for texts by Lennart Hellsing he shows himself to be an equal partner to this well-known writer. (p. 111)

PP und sein grosses Horn. Oetinger, 1958. *Getauscht ist getauscht*. Oetinger, 1960. Hellsing, L. *The cantankerous crow*. Blond, 1961.

STUPICA, Marlenka. Finished her art training at Ljubljana in 1950. She has illustrated painting-books, greeting cards, and many children's books, and her work appears in two children's magazines. In the course of twelve years she has five times been awarded prizes. Besides illustrating books by Yugoslavian authors she has also illustrated a volume of Grimm, *Pinocchio*, and a book each by Astrid Lindgren and Marcel Aymé. (p. 40)

Der Hirt. Mladinska, 1958; Atlantis, 1967; translated as *The magic ring*. World, 1968. Krüss, J. *Frosch und Vogel*. Kinderbuchverlag, 1964.

TANNINEN, Oili. Born 1933 in Sortavala, Finland, lives in Helsinki; gained a diploma in ceramics at the Helsinki school of industrial design. She has made designs for porcelain ware, drawn fairy-tale films for Finnish television and illustrated fairy-tales of her own invention. (p. 83)

TISDALL, Hans. Born 1910 in Munich, now lives in England and works as a designer, painter, and book illustrator. (p. 184)

Balbus, a picture-book of building. Pleiades, 1944; Transatlantic, 1945. *Wheels*. Pleiades, 1946. Allan, G. *Goosy Gander plays his part*. Muller, 1946.

TRIER, Walter. Born 1890 in Prague, died 1951 in Toronto. His life is marked by three new beginnings; first in Prague where, despite a gift for sport, he commenced his artistic training which he continued at Munich. Second, at the age of twenty, when he became a cartoonist and made drawings for the satirical magazine *Simplizissimus*, working also as an advertising artist and stage designer. It was during this period that he made the drawings for the children's books by Erich Kästner which have been reproduced in most of the translated editions. The first, *Emil*, appeared in 1928. In 1936 he left Germany for England where he worked for ten years, helping among other things to design the outward appearance of the magazine *Lilliput*. The last four years of his life were spent in Canada, where his name was little known but where he won much admiration for his graphic work in advertising and for his illustrations. (p. 90)

Kästner, E. *Till Eulenspiegel*. Atrium, 1938. Translated as *Eleven merry pranks of Till the jester*. Longmans, 1938, and as *Till Eulenspiegel*. Cape, 1967. *The jolly picnic*. Sylvan, 1944. Harris, J. C. *Brer Rabbit*. Penguin, 1945. *Das Eselein Dandy*. Schweizer Spiegel, 1948. Kästner, E. *Die Konferenz der Tiere*. Europa, 1949. Translated as *The animals' conference*. McKay, 1949; Collins, 1955. Kästner, E. *Der gestiefelte Kater*. Atrium, 1950. Translated as *Puss in boots*. Messner, 1957; Cape, 1967. Kästner, E. *Münchhausen*. Atrium, 1951. *Zehn kleine Negerlein*. Blüchert, 1953. *Muli das Zirkuseselchen*. Blüchert, 1954.

TRNKA, Jiři. Born 1912 in Pilsen, lives in Prague. As a child he used to carve puppets and design costumes for them, and a course in art at Prague increased his skill. As an adult he opened a puppet theatre, drew cartoons for the press and created some world-famous puppet films and cartoon films—both in colour and in black and white. He also illustrated children's books, usually by lithography, putting the coloured inks on to the stone himself. The singular features of his illustrations lie in their drama and their characterization; the figures may look like portly round puppets, but in spite of this they all possess a character of their own. (p. 99)

Hrubin, F. *Bitte, bitte noch ein Märchen*. Artia, 1955. *Rotkäppchen*. Artia, 1956. Andersen, H. C. *Fairy tales*. Hamlyn, 1959. Grimm, J. and W. *Fairy tales*. Hamlyn, 1961. Nezval, V. *Goldne Jugendzeit*. Artia, 1961. Branislav, F.

Musikanten, eilt herbei . . . Artia, 1962. La Fontaine, J. *Fables.* Hamlyn, 1962. *Through the magic gate.* Hamlyn, 1963. Hrubin, F. *Primrose and the winter witch.* Hamlyn, 1964. Prokofiev, S. *Peter and the wolf.* Hamlyn, 1965.
BIOG. Boček, J. *Jiří Trnka artist and puppet master.* Hamlyn, 1965.

TWO ARROWS, Tom. Belongs to the Iroquois tribe of Indians. Paintings of his are to be found in art galleries; he has created printed fabrics and greetings cards in a style very much his own. He has illustrated various books of which *Little boy Navajo* was the first in colour. In this and through his visits to schools, where he tells stories, draws, sings, and dances, he is attempting to arouse an understanding for the American Indian. (p. 137)

Bulla, C. R. *Eagle feather.* Crowell, 1953. Smiley, V. K. *Little boy Navajo.* Abelard, 1954.

UNGERER, Tomi. Born 1931 in Strassburg, lives in New York. He rejected various careers, made his way through Europe as a casual labourer and did his military service in the French camel corps; in 1957 he travelled to America. Self-taught, he started to paint and to illustrate, also drawing cartoons in which he converted his ideas into pictures with great rapidity. As a creator of picture-books he has shown considerable versatility and in his two books, *Snail, where are you?* and *One two where is my shoe?*, he is trying to encourage children to sketch and make designs for themselves. (pp. 117 and 170)

The Mellops go flying. Harper, 1957; Methuen, 1962. (And other titles.) *Crictor.* Harper, 1958; Methuen, 1959. *Rufus.* Harper, 1961. *Die drei Räuber.* Lentz, 1961. Translated as *The three robbers.* Atheneum, 1962; Methuen, 1964. *Snail, where are you?* Harper, 1962. Cole, W. *Frances face-maker.* World, 1963. *One two where is my shoe?* Harper, 1964. *Orlando the brave vulture.* Harper, 1966; Methuen, 1967. Brenner, B. *Mr. Tall and Mr. Small.* Scott, 1966; Oliver and Boyd, 1967. *Der Mondmann.* Diogenes, 1966. Translated as *Moon man.* Harper, 1966.

UNGERMANN, Arne. Born 1902 in Odense, lives in Copenhagen; after apprenticeship as a lithographer he worked for a newspaper in Odense. By 1930 he had moved to Copenhagen where he joined the permanent staff of the newspaper *Politiken* whose four-colour Sunday supplement afforded him great possibilities for developing his ideas. His picture-books with their imaginative illustrations stand at the peak of his creative work. (p. 144)

Sigsgaard, J. *Palle alene i Verden.* Copenhagen, 1942. Translated as *Paul alone in the world.* O.U.P., 1947. Sigsgaard, J. *Katinka und der Puppenwagen.* Oetinger, 1959. Translated as *Kathy and the doll buggy.* McGraw, 1961.

VASNETSOV, Yuri Alexeyevich. Born 1900 in Vyatka, lives in Russia; 1922 began to study art at the Leningrad Academy as a pupil of, among others, Lebedev (see p. 206). Since 1929 he has illustrated some eighty picture-books for children, chiefly Russian folk-tales such as Tolstoy's version of *The three bears* (which Lebedev also illustrated) in 1950 (see p. 127). He has also been the artistic director of a state toy-institute. (p. 79)

VICTOR, Paul-Emile. Born 1907 in Geneva. He is an ethnographer and polar explorer and has spent most of his life leading expeditions, flying, and soldiering in the polar regions. His *Apoutsiak, le petit flocon de neige* (p. 129) has therefore sprung from a deep knowledge of the subject, demonstrated in adult terms in his *Man and the conquest of the poles.* (Simon, 1963; Hamilton, 1965.)

VOGELNIK, Marija. Born 1914 in Ljubljana, lives in Yugoslavia. She received a diploma in architecture at Ljubljana and afterwards studied at the Academy of art in Belgrade. She regards the graphic problems of illustrating children's books as a special interest. A compilation of books which she has illustrated shows that she has a preference for songs and fairy stories. (p. 165)

WEIGEL, Susi. Born 1917 at Prossnitz, Moravia, lives in Austria. She was trained at the Academy of Applied Art in Vienna and subsequently drew for daily papers and periodicals. For a long time she was chief draughtsman for a company making cartoon films in Berlin. Her married name is Mair, but her children's books, which have received special awards on several occasions, are all published under her maiden name. (p. 141)

Lobe, M. *Hänschen Klein.* Jungbrunnen, 1954. Lobe, M. *Hannes und sein Bumpam.* Jugend u. Volk, 1961. Lobe, M. *Bimbulli.* Jungbrunnen, 1965.

WEISGARD, Leonard. Born 1916 at New Haven, Connecticut, lives at Roxbury in the same State; spent a year of his childhood in England, where picture-books made a considerable impression on him. He went to school in America and later studied modern dance, but could not support himself in this profession. He was keen to write and illustrate books for children, and modelled his style on early Bible illustrations, African cave painting, and early Russian and French picture-books. In over 150 children's books he has demonstrated his need to go on creating something new, and has shown his ability to get through to children (including his own) without talking down to them. He received the 1947 Caldecott Medal for *The little island.* (p. 149)

Suki the Siamese pussy, 1937. *Cinderella,* 1938. Brown, M. W. *The noisy books.* Scott and Harper, 1939–51. *The comical tragedy of Punch and Judy.* Scott, 1940. Macdonald, G. *Red light, green light.* Doubleday, 1944. Williams, G. *Timid Timothy.* Scott, 1944. Macdonald, G. *The little island.* Doubleday, 1946. Tresselt, A. *Rain drop splash.* Lothrop, 1946. *Down Huckleberry Hill.* Scribner, 1947. *The golden egg book.* Simon, 1947. *Family Mother Goose.* Harper, 1951. Fitch, F. M. *A book about God.* Lothrop, 1953. Joslin, S. *Brave baby elephant.* Harcourt, 1960; Collins, 1961. (And other titles.) Haviland, V. *Favourite tales told in Norway.* Little, 1961. Lewis, G. *When I go to the moon.* Macmillan, N.Y., 1961. Johnston, J. *Penguin's way.* Doubleday, 1962.
BIB. Miller, 445; Viguers, 249.
BIOG. Viguers, 197; Caldecott (1) by the Hurds; Kunitz, 293.
CRIT. *Contemporary art and children's book illustration* in HB (April 1960) by the artist himself.

WIKLAND, Ilon. Born 1930 at Dorpat, Esthonia, lives in Stockholm; works as a freelance artist and is the mother of three small children. She has illustrated books for the eights to twelves by Astrid Lindgren, Hans Peterson, Edith Unnerstad, and other authors. (p. 23)

Peterson, Hans. The *Magnus* books. Pantheon; Burke, 1959–. Lindgren, A. *Brenda Brave helps grandmother.* Webster, 1961; Burke, 1966. Falk, A. M. *Matthew comes to town.* Burke, 1966. (And other books in the 'Read for fun' series.) Lindgren, A. *Madicken.* O.U.P., 1963; translated as *Mischievous Meg.* Viking, 1962.

WILDSMITH, Brian. Born 1930 at Penistone, Yorkshire, lives in London. Son of a miner he might himself have become a miner, but won a scholarship to the Slade where he studied drawing and painting. He now combines his work as an illustrator with teaching at the Maidstone College of Art. He takes great pains over his illustrations, attempting not only to expand upon the text but also to give each picture a beauty and life of its own. His development from book illustrator and jacket designer to a picture-book artist took place through an edition of the *Arabian Nights* which appeared in 1961. This was followed by his first picture-book, the very impressive *ABC* for which he gained the Kate Greenaway Medal. Since then he has produced one or two fine picture-books every year and is gaining an ever-increasing international reputation. (colour illus., p. 28; and 103)

Brian Wildsmith's ABC, 1962. La Fontaine J. de. *The lion and the rat*, 1963. La Fontaine, J. de. *The North wind and the sun*, 1964. *Mother Goose*, 1964. *Brian Wildsmith's 123*, 1965. La Fontaine, J. de. *The rich man and the shoemaker*, 1965. La Fontaine, J. de. *The hare and the tortoise*, 1966. *Birds by Brian Wildsmith*, and *Wild Animals by Brian Wildsmith*, 1967. (All O.U.P. and Watts.)
BIOG. JB (July 1963) by Marcus Crouch. Ryder, 122–3.

WILKOŃ, Józef. Born 1930 at Wieliczka, Poland, lives in Poland; 1949–55 studied painting, graphic art and history of art. His pictures have often been exhibited and his book illustrations (he has a great liking for Rabelais, Rilke, and Cervantes) have gained two prizes. His children's books have emerged in a back to front way—the pictures first, for which he then attempts to find an author. (p. 190)

Schaaf, P. *The crane with one leg*. Warne, 1964. Valentin, U. *Mr. Minkepatt and his friends*. Dobson, 1965.

WILLIAMS, Garth Montgomery. Born 1912 in New York, lives at Aspen, Colorado. His parents were both artists and his childhood and student years were spent in England. During his training he found himself more and more drawn to sculpture and in 1936 he won the British Prix de Rome for his work in this field. During his stay in England he also helped in the establishment of the School of Art at Luton and worked at murals. In 1941 he returned to America and worked for a while for the *New Yorker*. A commission to illustrate E. B. White's *Stuart Little* (1945) turned his attention to children's books and he is now very active in this field and has developed a marked style of his own (particularly noticeable in his fine drawing of animals). (p. 65)

Tall book of make believe. Harper, 1950; Ward, 1959. Moore, L. *My first counting book*. Simon, 1957; Purnell, n.d. (And other board-books.) *The rabbits' wedding*. Harper, 1958; Collins, 1960. Zolotow, C. *Do you know what I'll do?* Harper, 1958. Hoban, R. *Bedtime for Frances*. Harper, 1960; Faber, 1963. Zolotow, C. *The sky was blue*. Harper, 1963.
BIB. Viguers, 250.
BIOG. Mahony, 372–3; Viguers, 200; Fuller, 227.
CRIT. HB (December 1953) by the artist; HB (June 1961) by Rita Fara.

WINTER, Klaus and BISCHOFF, Helmut. Born respectively 1928 at Frankfurt a.M. and 1926 at Seckach, both live in Germany; Winter was trained at various schools of art, Bischoff completed an apprenticeship to an architect. They got to know each other at the Karlsruhe Academy of fine arts and worked together in poster design and advertising. In 1958 they produced their first picture-book, which was notable for the way in which it united the techniques of the painter and the graphic artist. (p. 66)

Mauersberger, H. *Die Sonne*. Maier, 1958. Hoytema, T. v. *Die glücklichen Eulen*. Lentz/Beltz, 1962. *Mool*. Herder, 1962. *Hoppla-Hoppla Bauersmann*. Beltz, 1964. Translated as *Hoppla hoppla farmerman*. Children's, 1966. *Happy Owls*. Lion Press, 1967.

YAMAMOTO, Tadayoshi. Born 1916 in Tokyo; illustrated books for children while still at school and later completed a course in drawing. His liking for children and for all kinds of mechanical transport coincide in the most lively way in his picture-books. (pp. 188–9).

YAMANAKA, Haruo. Born in Osaka, died 1962. Before the war he went to Manchuria and afterwards travelled to France, living for a time in Paris. Gifted with a sense of fantasy and a rich imagination, he liked best to illustrate the authors of fairy-tales. (p. 122)

ZÁBRANSKÝ, Adolf. Born 1909 in Rybí, lives in Prague. His artistic training at two different schools was followed by a longish period in which he devoted himself chiefly to oil-painting. Several of his works, among which murals and graffiti can also be numbered, have been awarded prizes. As a graphic artist he has illustrated mainly for newspapers and the producers of picture-books. Without doubt it is entirely due to his illustrations that various collections of verse by well-known Czech poets have been translated into German and other languages. (p. 88)

Ćarek, J. *Ráj domova*. Hynek, 1946. Adapted as *Underneath my apple tree*. Lippincott, 1960. Denk, P. *Do kola*. SNDK, 1951. Adapted as *Ring o'roses*. Dakers, 1958; and *Ring-a-ling*. Lippincott, 1959. Hrubin, F. *Slcecný usmev*. Mlada leta, 1960. Adapted as *The smiling sun*. Hamlyn, 1961.
BIB. and BIOG. JB (December 1964) by J. Dohm.

ZACHARIAS, Wanda. Born 1931 in Munich, lives on the Starnberger lake; studied at the Munich Academy as a pupil of Professor Praetorius and an advanced student under Professor Seewald. She also studied theatre arts and literature for six semesters at Munich University. Her husband, Dr. Thomas Zacharias, offers ideas and drawings which play a part in her work on picture-books. (p. 167)

Pocci, F. *Kasperls Reise übers Meer*. Mohn, 1960. Zacharias, T. *Mikosch, das Karussellpferd*. Mohn, 1962. Baumann, H. *Tina und Nina*. Mohn, 1963. Translated under the same title. O.U.P., 1963. *Und wo ist der grüne Papagei?* Mohn, 1965.

ZIMNIK, Reiner. Born 1930 in Beuthen, Upper Silesia, lives in Munich; was an apprentice joiner before leaving to study art. As a student he was given the opportunity to illustrate a story, but since he was dissatisfied with its content he replaced it with a story of his own. This he illustrated and *Xaver der Ringelstecher* was born. Since that time his own texts have formed the foundation for his black-and-white picture-books, which, although full of humour and imagination, are not directed exclusively at children. For instance, there is the constantly recurring figure of Lektro, the little man struggling to live a life of his own in a world of technology. Like other Zimnik figures before him, he is also to be seen on the television. Only in 1958 did Zimnik's first picture-book appear in colour. (p. 172)

Xaver der Ringelstecher. Parcus, 1954. *Jonas der Angler*. Parcus, 1954. Translated as *Jonas the fisherman*. Pantheon, 1956; Faber, 1957. *Der Kran*. Dressler, 1956. *Die Trommler für eine bessere Zeit*. Zürich, 1958. Translated as *Drummers of dreams*. Faber, 1960. Axmann, H. *Die Geschichte vom Käuzchen*. Diogenes, 1960. Translated as *The little owl*. Methuen, 1960; Atheneum, 1962. Baumann, H. *Der Bär auf dem Motorrad*. Diogenes, 1962. Translated as *The bear on the motor-cycle*. O.U.P.; Atheneum, 1963.

ZINGER, Oleg. Born 1909 in Moscow, lives in Paris. He has been influenced by life in three countries; Russia where he spent his childhood up to 1922, Germany where he received his training in art from 1926–31, and France where he has settled today. His picture-book illustrations have been made and printed chiefly in Germany. (p. 73)

Windmüller, I. *Ist das ein Löwe?* Kinderbuchverlag, 1950. Windmüller, I. *Er heisst Jakob*. Kinderbuchverlag, 1951. Translated as *Little donkey*. McGraw, 1959.

Some Further Reading and Sources of Information

General: Mrs. Hürlimann discusses many aspects of children's book illustration in her *Three centuries of children's books in Europe* (London, Oxford University Press, 1967; Cleveland, World, 1968) and the book includes bibliographical notes on European source material in various languages. Fuller bibliographies, especially of American books, are given in several sections of *Children's literature: a guide to reference sources*, prepared under the direction of Virginia Haviland for the Library of Congress (Washington, 1966). But the fullest general treatment of the subject is undoubtedly Horn Book Incorporated's *Illustrators of children's books 1744–1945* and its *Supplement* covering the years 1946–56 (Boston, 1947 and 1958). The biographical sections of these volumes have been supplemented a little by entries on illustrators in *The junior book of authors*, edited by Stanley J. Kunitz and Howard Haycraft, and *More junior authors*, edited by Muriel Fuller (New York, H. W. Wilson, 1951 and 1963).

History: Richly illustrated and containing an extensive bibliography, David Bland's *A history of book illustration* is much the fullest survey of the whole subject (London, Faber; Cleveland, World, 1958). It apportions due place to children's books, which are also discussed in more limited historical studies such as Ruari McLean's *Victorian book design* (London, Faber; New York, Oxford University Press, 1963) and John Lewis's *The twentieth century book: its illustration and design* (London, Studio Vista; New York, Reinhold, 1967).

Several standard histories of children's literature also describe the development of illustration as an integral part of their theme, but none gives the wealth of example that was in Percy Muir's *English children's books 1600–1900* (London, Batsford; New York, Praeger, 1954), now out of print. Charles H. Morris's pamphlet, *The illustration of children's books* (London, The Library Association, 1957), gives a brief introduction, but without the enthusiasm and attractiveness of such an introductory study as Janet Adam Smith's *Children's illustrated books* (London, Collins, 1948), which is also out of print.

Technique: It is not always easy to separate books on illustration processes from those on illustration as an art—books like David Bland's *The illustration of books* (third edition, London, Faber, 1962) and Henry Pitz's *Illustrating children's books* (New York, Watson-Guptill, 1963) combining both aspects of the subject.

Perhaps the best introduction to processes, however, is Sean Jennet's *The making of books* (fourth edition, London, Faber; New York, Praeger, 1967), while a more detailed technical survey, intended for 'the layman', is Harold Curwen's *Processes of graphic reproduction* (fourth edition revised by Charles Mayo, London, 1967). Lynton Lamb has provided the student illustrator with a useful introduction to principles, processes and business arrangements in his *Drawing for illustration* (London; New York, Oxford University Press, 1962), and John Ryder's *Artists of a certain line* (London, Bodley Head, 1960; Pennsylvania, Dufour, 1961), while principally a set of biographies, gives some notes on the techniques and methods of work of the illustrators included. A notable series of technical articles by illustrators themselves appeared in Horn Book Magazine from 1963 onwards under the title of *The artist at work.*

Criticism: Very little systematic attention has been paid to picturebooks in child development. Perhaps the most stimulating assessments have been made by Lillian Smith in *The unreluctant years* (Chicago, American Library Association, 1953) and in Dorothy Neal White's two books, *About books for children* and *Books before five* (London, Oxford University Press, 1944 and 1954). Two articles in *The Penrose annual*, vol. 56 (London, Lund Humphries, 1962) pointed clearly to the need for a more child-oriented view of graphic design, but detailed criticism on such principles is to be found mostly among the columns of the reviewing journals. Two of the liveliest of those in current issue are *Growing point*, edited and largely written by Margery Fisher (Northampton, May 1962+), and *Children's book news*, edited by Nancy Lockwood (London, Children's Book Centre, May 1964+); but *Horn Book Magazine* (Boston, Horn Book Incorporated, 1924+) and *Junior bookshelf* (Huddersfield, Woodfield & Stanley, 1936+) must be singled out for their long-lived dedication to the achievement of standards both in the writing and the criticism of children's books. In the international field, the magazine *Graphis* (Zürich, 1945+) has been responsible for many informative articles on picture-books and their illustrators, whole issues occasionally being devoted to this subject.

Awards: The start of an international clearing-house for ideas and criticism in children's books is to be seen in the work of the International Board on Books for Young People. Many of the awards mentioned in *Picture-book world* are announced or described in the Board's magazine *Bookbird* (Vienna, 1958+) and the International Youth Library at Munich has also issued a list of international awards in *Children's prize books* (Munich, 1963).

The most adequate national coverage of awards is in the U.S.A., where *Horn Book Magazine* regularly publishes biographical and bibliographical details of winners of the two main annual awards, together with their acceptance speeches. These have been cumulated in volume form—the two volumes dealing with the picture-book award being; *Caldecott medal books 1938–1957* (Boston, 1957), edited by Bertha Miller and Elinor Field, and *Newbery and Caldecott medal books 1956–1965*, edited by Lee Kingman (Boston, 1965).

Visual aids: Mention should finally be made of the growing number of publishers on both sides of the Atlantic who are making available exhibition material and charts to demonstrate how artists and printers set about the creation of modern picture-books. The Children's Services Division of the American Library Association was also responsible for commissioning from Weston Woods Studios, Connecticut, a one-hour film on *The lively art of picture-books* (1964)—a harbinger of some lively mechanics in the conversion of original picture-books into material for films and film-strips.

B.W.A.

Index

Reference is made here only to the artists and subjects touched on in the text of the Introduction and of the Picture Section. Cross-referencing within the book indicates artists whose work is illustrated or who are given fuller treatment in the Bio-bibliographical Supplement.